Contents

Cookie

Pumpkin Brownies

Prep: 20 mins **Cook:** 40 mins **Total:** 1 hr **Servings:** 16 **Yield:** 1 - 8x8 inch pan of brownies

Ingredients

- ¾ cup all-purpose flour
- ½ teaspoon baking powder
- ½ teaspoon salt
- ¾ cup butter, melted
- 1 ½ cups white sugar
- 2 teaspoons vanilla extract
- 3 large eggs eggs

- ¼ cup cocoa powder
- ½ cup semi-sweet chocolate chips
- ½ cup pumpkin puree
- ½ cup chopped walnuts
- ¾ teaspoon ground cinnamon
- ½ teaspoon ground cloves
- ½ teaspoon ground nutmeg

Directions

Step 1

Preheat oven to 350 degrees F (175 degrees C). Grease an 8x8 inch baking pan. Stir the flour, baking powder, and salt together in a bowl.

Step 2

In another bowl, stir together the melted butter, sugar, and vanilla extract; beat in the eggs one at a time with a spoon. Gradually add the flour mixture, and stir the batter until it's evenly moistened. Divide the batter in half in two separate bowls.

Step 3

Into one bowl of batter, blend the cocoa powder and chocolate chips. In the second bowl of batter, stir in the pumpkin puree, walnuts, cinnamon, cloves, and nutmeg.

Step 4

Spread 1/2 of the chocolate batter into the bottom of the prepared baking pan, and follow with 1/2 of the pumpkin batter. Repeat the layers, ending with a pumpkin layer, and drag a kitchen knife or small spatula gently through the layers in a swirling motion, to create a marbled appearance.

Step 5

Bake in the preheated oven until the brownies begin to pull away from the sides of the pan, and a toothpick inserted into the center comes out clean, 40 to 45 minutes. Cool in the pan, cut into squares, and serve.

Nutrition Facts

Per Serving:

241.5 calories; protein 3g 6% DV; carbohydrates 28.8g 9% DV; fat 13.9g 21% DV; cholesterol 57.8mg 19% DV; sodium 182mg 7% DV.

Spooky Witches' Fingers

Prep: 35 mins **Cook:** 20 mins **Additional:** 20 mins **Total:** 1 hr 15 mins **Servings:** 60 **Yield:** 60 cookies

Ingredients

- 1 cup butter, softened
- 1 cup confectioners' sugar
- 1 egg
- 1 teaspoon almond extract
- 1 teaspoon vanilla extract

- 2 ⅔ cups all-purpose flour
- 1 teaspoon baking powder
- 1 teaspoon salt
- ¾ cup whole almonds
- 1 (.75 ounce) tube red decorating gel

Directions

Step 1

Combine the butter, sugar, egg, almond extract, and vanilla extract in a mixing bowl. Beat together with an electric mixer; gradually add the flour, baking powder, and salt, continually beating; refrigerate 20 to 30 minutes.

Step 2

Preheat oven to 325 degrees F (165 degrees C). Lightly grease baking sheets.

Step 3

Remove dough from refrigerator in small amounts. Scoop 1 heaping teaspoon at a time onto a piece of waxed paper. Use the waxed paper to roll the dough into a thin finger-shaped cookie. Press one almond into one end of each cookie to give the appearance of a long fingernail. Squeeze cookie near the tip and again near the center of each to give the impression of knuckles. You can also cut into the dough with a sharp knife at the same points to help give a more finger-like appearance. Arrange the shaped cookies on the baking sheets.

Step 4

Bake in the preheated oven until the cookies are slightly golden in color, 20 to 25 minutes.

Step 5

Remove the almond from the end of each cookie; squeeze a small amount of red decorating gel into the cavity; replace the almond to cause the gel to ooze out around the tip of the cookie.

Nutrition Facts

Per Serving:

68.3 calories; protein 1.1g 2% DV; carbohydrates 6.9g 2% DV; fat 4.1g 6% DV; cholesterol 11.2mg 4% DV; sodium 75.7mg 3% DV.

Halloween Chocolate Chip Cookies with Spiders

Prep: 30 mins **Cook:** 11 mins **Additional:** 1 min **Total:** 42 mins **Servings:** 48 **Yield:** 4 dozen

Ingredients

- 2 ½ cups all-purpose flour
- 1 teaspoon baking soda
- 1 teaspoon salt
- ½ teaspoon baking powder
- 1 cup unsalted butter, at room temperature
- ¾ cup white sugar
- ¾ cup packed brown sugar
- 2 large eggs eggs
- 1 teaspoon vanilla extract
- 2 ½ cups semisweet chocolate chips, divided

Directions

Step 1

Preheat oven to 350 degrees F (175 degrees C).

Step 2

Combine flour, baking soda, salt, and baking powder in a large bowl and stir with a fork to mix ingredients well.

Step 3

Combine butter, white sugar, and brown sugar in a large bowl; beat with an electric mixer until smooth and creamy. Add eggs and vanilla extract and beat until smooth and fluffy. Add in flour mixture, 1 cup at a time, and mix in with a spatula until well incorporated. Fold in 1 1/2 cups chocolate chips until well combined.

Step 4

Drop cookies onto ungreased baking sheets. Pour 1/2 cup chocolate chips into a bowl. Push about 3 to 4 chocolate chips onto each cookie, tip-side down, to make the spider bodies.

Step 5

Bake in the the preheated oven until edges are golden, 10 to 15 minutes. Cool on the baking sheet for 1 minute before removing to a wire rack.

Step 6

Melt remaining 1/2 cup chocolate in a microwave-safe glass or ceramic bowl in 15-second intervals, stirring after each melting, 1 to 3 minutes. Spoon melted chocolate into a piping bag with a small tip and draw little legs on each side of the spider bodies to create spider legs.

Nutrition Facts

Per Serving:

127.9 calories; protein 1.3g 3% DV; carbohydrates 17g 6% DV; fat 6.7g 10% DV; cholesterol 17.9mg 6% DV; sodium 112mg 5% DV.

Witches' Hats

Prep: 1 hr **Total:** 1 hr **Servings:** 32 **Yield:** 32 servings

Ingredients

- 2 (16 ounce) packages fudge stripe cookies
- ¼ cup honey, or as needed
- 1 (9 ounce) bag milk chocolate candy kisses, unwrapped
- 1 (4.5 ounce) tube decorating gel

Directions

Step 1

Place a fudge stripe cookie with bottom side up onto a work surface. Smear a small dab (about 1/8 teaspoon) of honey onto the bottom of a chocolate kiss, and secure the candy piece to the center of the cookie, covering the hole. Use decorating gel to pipe a small bow onto the cookie at the base of the candy piece. Repeat with remaining ingredients.

Nutrition Facts

Per Serving:

203.7 calories; protein 2.4g 5% DV; carbohydrates 28.5g 9% DV; fat 8.7g 13% DV; cholesterol 1.7mg 1% DV; sodium 169.9mg 7% DV.

Sugar Cookie Icing

Prep: 15 mins **Total:** 15 mins **Servings:** 12 **Yield:** 1 dozen cookies' worth

Ingredients

- 1 cup confectioners' sugar
- 2 teaspoons milk
- 2 teaspoons light corn syrup
- ¼ teaspoon almond extract
- Recommended:
- assorted food coloring

Directions

Step 1

In a small bowl, stir together confectioners' sugar and milk until smooth. Beat in corn syrup and almond extract until icing is smooth and glossy. If icing is too thick, add more corn syrup.

Step 2

Divide into separate bowls, and add food colorings to each to desired intensity. Dip cookies, or paint them with a brush.

Nutrition Facts

Per Serving:

42.4 calories; proteing; carbohydrates 10.8g 4% DV; fatg; cholesterolmg; sodium 0.8mg.

Halloween Skeleton Cookies

Prep: 45 mins **Cook:** 8 mins **Additional:** 6 hrs 20 mins **Total:** 7 hrs 13 mins **Servings:** 40 **Yield:** 40 cookies

Ingredients

- 1 ½ cups white sugar
- 1 cup butter, softened
- 2 eaches eggs
- 1 ½ teaspoons vanilla extract
- 1 ½ teaspoons almond flavoring
- 3 ½ cups all-purpose flour
- 1 teaspoon baking powder
- ½ teaspoon salt
- 2 tablespoons confectioners' sugar

Icing:

- 1 cup confectioners' sugar
- 2 teaspoons milk, plus more as needed
- 2 teaspoons light corn syrup, or more as needed
- ¼ teaspoon vanilla extract
- 1 (1.5 ounce) tube black decorating gel

Directions

Step 1

Cream sugar and butter in a bowl with an electric mixer until creamy. Add eggs, 1 1/2 teaspoons vanilla extract, and almond flavoring and mix well.

Step 2

Stir flour, baking powder, and salt together in a second bowl. Add flour mixture to the creamed butter mixture and mix to combine. Wrap in plastic wrap and chill in the refrigerator for 3 to 4 hours or overnight.

Step 3

Preheat oven to 350 degrees F (175 degrees C). Line 2 baking sheets with parchment paper.

Step 4

Dust a work surface with 2 tablespoons confectioners' sugar and roll out dough into a 1/4-inch-thick circle. Cut out figure shapes with a gingerbread man cookie cutter and arrange cut-out cookies on prepared baking sheets.

Step 5

Bake in the preheated oven for 8 to 10 minutes. Remove from baking sheets carefully and transfer to wire racks. Cool completely, about 20 minutes.

Step 6

Stir 1 cup confectioners' sugar and milk together in a small bowl until smooth. Beat in corn syrup and 1/4 teaspoon vanilla extract until icing is smooth and glossy. Add more corn syrup if icing is too thick.

Step 7

Spoon icing into a piping bag with a small plain tip. Draw a filled-out circle inside the head for the skull and a skeleton on the body, including 3 horizontal lines for the ribs. Let cookies stand until icing dries completely, about 2 hour, best overnight.

Step 8

Use black decorating gel to draw eyes, a nose, and a mouth on the skull and let cookies dry again, about 1 hour.

Nutrition Facts

Per Serving:

131.2 calories; protein 1.5g 3% DV; carbohydrates 20.4g 7% DV; fat 4.9g 8% DV; cholesterol 20.4mg 7% DV; sodium 94.5mg 4% DV.

Apple Crisp Cookies

Prep: 30 mins **Cook:** 10 mins **Additional:** 50 mins **Total:** 1 hr 30 mins **Servings:** 24 **Yield:** 2 dozen cookies

Ingredients

- 2 cups whole wheat flour, plus
- 2 tablespoons whole wheat flour
- 1 ½ teaspoons ground cinnamon
- 1 tcaspoon baking powder
- 1 teaspoon salt
- ½ cup butter, softened
- ½ cup demerara sugar
- ½ cup brown sugar
- 7 tablespoons apple butter
- 2 large eggs eggs
- 1 teaspoon vanilla extract
- 3 tablespoons apple juice

- 2 cups quick cooking oats
- 1 apple, finely chopped

Directions

Step 1

Preheat oven to 375 degrees F (190 degrees C). In a large bowl, mix all of the whole wheat flour together with the cinnamon, baking powder and salt.

Step 2

In a separate bowl, mash the butter, demerara sugar, and brown sugar together until thoroughly combined, then stir in the apple butter until smooth. Stir in eggs, vanilla extract, and apple juice until well mixed; pour the liquid mixture into the flour mixture about 1/3 cup at a time, stirring after each addition. Mix in the oats and chopped apple.

Step 3

With 2 teaspoons, form the dough into balls and place onto ungreased baking sheets about 2 inches apart.

Step 4

Bake in the preheated oven until the cookies are lightly browned and set in the centers, about 10 minutes; allow to cool for about 2 minutes on baking sheets until removing to finish cooling on wire racks.

Nutrition Facts

Per Serving:

147.6 calories; protein 3g 6% DV; carbohydrates 24.1g 8% DV; fat 4.9g 8% DV; cholesterol 25.7mg 9% DV; sodium 155mg 6% DV.

Pumpkin Cookies III

Prep: 15 mins **Cook:** 15 mins **Total:** 30 mins **Servings:** 36 **Yield:** 3 dozen

Ingredients

- 1 cup white sugar
- 1 egg
- 1 cup shortening
- 1 teaspoon vanilla extract
- 2 cups all-purpose flour
- 1 teaspoon baking soda
- 1 teaspoon baking powder
- 1 teaspoon salt
- 1 teaspoon ground cinnamon
- 1 cup canned pumpkin
- ½ cup raisins
- ½ cup chopped walnuts

Directions

Step 1

Preheat oven to 350 degrees F (175 degrees C). Grease cookie sheets.

Step 2

In a large bowl, cream together sugar, egg, shortening, and vanilla. Sift together flour, baking soda, baking powder, salt, and cinnamon; stir into the creamed mixture. Stir in the pumpkin, raisins, and walnuts. Drop dough by teaspoonfuls onto the prepared cookie sheets.

Step 3

Bake 10-15 minutes in the preheated oven.

Nutrition Facts

Per Serving:

119.5 calories; protein 1.3g 3% DV; carbohydrates 13.6g 4% DV; fat 7g 11% DV; cholesterol 5.2mg 2% DV; sodium 131.9mg 5% DV.

Iced Pumpkin Cookies

Prep: 20 mins **Cook:** 20 mins **Additional:** 40 mins **Total:** 1 hr 20 mins **Servings:** 36 **Yield:** 3 dozen

Ingredients

- 2 ½ cups all-purpose flour
- 1 teaspoon baking powder
- 1 teaspoon baking soda
- 2 teaspoons ground cinnamon
- ½ teaspoon ground nutmeg
- ½ teaspoon ground cloves
- ½ teaspoon salt
- ½ cup butter, softened
- 1 ½ cups white sugar
- 1 cup canned pumpkin puree
- 1 egg
- 1 teaspoon vanilla extract
- 2 cups confectioners' sugar
- 3 tablespoons milk
- 1 tablespoon melted butter
- 1 teaspoon vanilla extract

Directions

Step 1

Preheat oven to 350 degrees F (175 degrees C). Combine flour, baking powder, baking soda, cinnamon, nutmeg, ground cloves, and salt; set aside.

Step 2

In a medium bowl, cream together the 1/2 cup of butter and white sugar. Add pumpkin, egg, and 1 teaspoon vanilla to butter mixture, and beat until creamy. Mix in dry ingredients. Drop on cookie sheet by tablespoonfuls; flatten slightly.

Step 3

Bake for 15 to 20 minutes in the preheated oven. Cool cookies, then drizzle glaze with fork.

Step 4

To Make Glaze: Combine confectioners' sugar, milk, 1 tablespoon melted butter, and 1 teaspoon vanilla. Add milk as needed, to achieve drizzling consistency.

Nutrition Facts

Per Serving:

121.5 calories; protein 1.2g 3% DV; carbohydrates 22.4g 7% DV; fat 3.2g 5% DV; cholesterol 12.9mg 4% DV; sodium 120.5mg 5% DV.

Chocolate Mice

Prep: 20 mins **Additional:** 2 hrs **Total:** 2 hrs 20 mins **Servings:** 12 **Yield:** 1 dozen

Ingredients

- 4 (1 ounce) squares semisweet chocolate
- ⅓ cup sour cream
- 1 cup chocolate cookie crumbs
- ⅓ cup chocolate cookie crumbs
- ⅓ cup confectioners' sugar
- 24 eaches silver dragees decorating candy
- ¼ cup sliced almonds
- 12 (2 inch) pieces long red vine licorice

Directions

Step 1

Melt the chocolate, and combine with sour cream. Stir in 1 cup chocolate cookie crumbs. Cover and refrigerate until firm.

Step 2

Roll by level tablespoonfuls into balls. Mold to a slight point at one end (the nose).

Step 3

Roll dough in confectioners sugar (for white mice), and in chocolate cookie crumbs (for dark mice). On each mouse, place dragees in appropriate spot for eyes, almond slices for ears, and a licorice string for the tail.

Step 4

Refrigerate for at least two hours, until firm.

Nutrition Facts

Per Serving:

176.4 calories; protein 2.3g 5% DV; carbohydrates 27.4g 9% DV; fat 7.2g 11% DV; cholesterol 3.1mg 1% DV; sodium 89.8mg 4% DV.

The Best Rolled Sugar Cookies

Prep: 20 mins **Cook:** 8 mins **Additional:** 2 hrs 32 mins **Total:** 3 hrs **Servings:** 60 **Yield:** 5 dozen

Ingredients

- 1 ½ cups butter, softened
- 2 cups white sugar
- 4 large eggs eggs
- 1 teaspoon vanilla extract
- 5 cups all-purpose flour
- 2 teaspoons baking powder
- 1 teaspoon salt

Directions

Step 1

In a large bowl, cream together butter and sugar until smooth. Beat in eggs and vanilla. Stir in the flour, baking powder, and salt. Cover, and chill dough for at least one hour (or overnight).

Step 2

Preheat oven to 400 degrees F (200 degrees C). Roll out dough on floured surface 1/4 to 1/2 inch thick. Cut into shapes with any cookie cutter. Place cookies 1 inch apart on ungreased cookie sheets.

Step 3

Bake 6 to 8 minutes in preheated oven. Cool completely.

Nutrition Facts

Per Serving:

109.5 calories; protein 1.5g 3% DV; carbohydrates 14.7g 5% DV; fat 5g 8% DV; cholesterol 24.6mg 8% DV; sodium 92.6mg 4% DV.

Acorn Candy Cookies

Prep: 15 mins **Additional:** 30 mins **Total:** 45 mins **Servings:** 24 **Yield:** 2 dozen acorns

Ingredients

- 1 tablespoon prepared chocolate frosting
- 24 piece (blank)s milk chocolate candy kisses (such as Hershey's Kisses), unwrapped
- 24 wafers mini vanilla wafer cookies (such as Nilla)
- 24 eaches butterscotch chips

Directions

Step 1

Smear a small amount of frosting onto the flat bottom of a candy kiss. Press onto the flat bottom of the vanilla wafer. Smear a little more frosting onto the flat bottom of a butterscotch chip, and press onto the rounded top of the cookie. Repeat with remaining ingredients. Set aside to dry, about 30 minutes.

Nutrition Facts

Per Serving:

132 calories; protein 0.5g 1% DV; carbohydrates 15.6g 5% DV; fat 6.7g 10% DV; cholesterol 1mg; sodium 31.5mg 1% DV.

Haunted Oreos

Prep: 15 mins **Additional:** 1 hr 15 mins **Total:** 1 hr 30 mins **Servings:** 26 **Yield:** 26 servings

Ingredients

- 12 ounces white chocolate chips
- 26 cookies chocolate sandwich cookies (such as Oreo)
- 6 ounces milk chocolate chips

Directions

Step 1

Line a baking sheet with parchment paper.

Step 2

Melt white chocolate in the top of a double boiler over simmering water, stirring frequently and scraping down the sides with a rubber spatula to avoid scorching.

Step 3

Dip each sandwich cookie in melted white chocolate to coat completely; transfer cookies to the prepared baking sheet. Chill in the freezer until almost hardened, about 30 minutes.

Step 4

Press 2 chocolate chips into each cookie to resemble eyes and 1 chocolate chip below the "eyes" to resemble a mouth. Chill in the freezer until completely set, about 45 minutes.

Nutrition Facts

Per Serving:

154 calories; protein 1.9g 4% DV; carbohydrates 18.3g 6% DV; fat 8.6g 13% DV; cholesterol 4.9mg 2% DV; sodium 72.7mg 3% DV.

Cake Balls

Prep: 40 mins **Cook:** 30 mins **Additional:** 2 hrs **Total:** 3 hrs 10 mins **Servings:** 36 **Yield:** 3 dozen

Ingredients

- 1 (18.25 ounce) package chocolate cake mix
- 1 (16 ounce) container prepared chocolate frosting
- 1 (3 ounce) bar chocolate flavored confectioners coating

Directions

Step 1

Prepare the cake mix according to package directions using any of the recommended pan sizes. When cake is done, crumble while warm into a large bowl, and stir in the frosting until well blended.

Step 2

Melt chocolate coating in a glass bowl in the microwave, or in a metal bowl over a pan of simmering water, stirring occasionally until smooth.

Step 3

Use a melon baller or small scoop to form balls of the chocolate cake mixture. Dip the balls in chocolate using a toothpick or fork to hold them. Place on waxed paper to set.

Nutrition Facts

Per Serving:

123.6 calories; protein 1.1g 2% DV; carbohydrates 19.7g 6% DV; fat 5.2g 8% DV; cholesterol 0.5mg; sodium 143.4mg 6% DV.

Halloween Ghost Cookies

Prep: 45 mins **Cook:** 6 mins **Additional:** 2 hrs 15 mins **Total:** 3 hrs 6 mins **Servings:** 90 **Yield:** 90 cookies

Ingredients

- 1 cup butter
- 1 ½ cups confectioners' sugar
- 1 egg
- 1 teaspoon vanilla extract
- 2 ½ cups all-purpose flour
- 1 teaspoon baking soda
- 1 teaspoon cream of tartar
- ¼ teaspoon salt

- Icing:
- 1 cup confectioners' sugar
- 2 teaspoons milk, plus more if needed
- 2 teaspoons light corn syrup, or more as needed
- ¼ teaspoon vanilla extract
- 1 (12 ounce) package miniature semisweet chocolate chips

Directions

Step 1

Beat butter in a bowl with an electric mixer until creamy. Add 1 1/2 cups confectioners' sugar gradually, beating until light and fluffy. Beat in egg and 1 teaspoon vanilla extract.

Step 2

Combine flour, baking soda, cream of tartar, and salt in a second bowl. Add flour mixture to the creamed butter mixture and mix to combine. Wrap in plastic wrap and chill in the refrigerator for at least 1 hour.

Step 3

Preheat oven to 400 degrees F (200 degrees C).

Step 4

Dust a work surface with flour and roll out dough into a thin circle. Cut out tulip shapes; if your tulip cookie cutter has a stem, cut the stem off with a knife, so you have a stemless tulip shape. Arrange cut-out cookies on ungreased baking sheets.

Step 5

Bake in the preheated oven until lightly browned, 6 to 8 minutes. Remove from baking sheets carefully and transfer to wire racks. Cool completely, about 15 minutes.

Step 6

Stir 1 cup confectioners' sugar and milk together in a small bowl until smooth. Beat in corn syrup and 1/4 teaspoon vanilla extract until icing is smooth and glossy. Add more corn syrup if icing is too thick.

Step 7

Spoon icing into a piping bag with a small plain tip. Pipe icing around the edge of each cookie to create a border. Fill in the middle completely with icing. Stick 2 chocolate chip cookies into the wet icing for the eyes. Let cookies stand until icing dries, about 1 hour.

Nutrition Facts

Per Serving:

63.5 calories; protein 0.6g 1% DV; carbohydrates 8.6g 3% DV; fat 3.3g 5% DV; cholesterol 7.5mg 3% DV; sodium 36.4mg 2% DV.

Michelle's Soft Sugar Cookies

Servings: 60 **Yield:** 3 to 5 dozen

Ingredients

- 1 cup margarine
- 1 ½ cups white sugar
- 3 large eggs eggs
- 1 teaspoon vanilla extract
- 3 ½ cups all-purpose flour
- 2 teaspoons cream of tartar
- 1 teaspoon baking soda
- ½ teaspoon salt

Directions

Step 1

Cream the margarine and add the sugar gradually. Beat until light and fluffy. Add eggs one at time, mixing well after each addition.

Step 2

Stir in the vanilla. Add the flour, cream of tartar, baking soda and salt gradually to the creamed mixture, stirring in by hand. Cover and chill dough overnight.

Step 3

Preheat oven to 375 degrees F (190 degrees C). Line baking sheets with parchment paper.

Step 4

Roll dough out on a floured surface to 1/8 to 1/4 inch thick and cut into your favorite shapes. Place cookies onto the prepared baking sheets.

Step 5

Bake at 375 degrees F (190 degrees C) for 6 to 8 minutes or until cookie has a golden appearance.

Nutrition Facts

Per Serving:

76.7 calories; protein 1.1g 2% DV; carbohydrates 10.7g 3% DV; fat 3.3g 5% DV; cholesterol 9.3mg 3% DV; sodium 79.1mg 3% DV.

Meringue Bones

Prep: 30 mins **Cook:** 1 hr **Additional:** 1 hr **Total:** 2 hrs 30 mins **Servings:** 36 **Yield:** 3 dozen bones

Ingredients

- 6 large egg whites egg whites
- ½ teaspoon cream of tartar
- 1 pinch salt

- 1 ⅓ cups white sugar
- 2 teaspoons vanilla extract

Directions

Step 1

Preheat oven to 225 degrees F (110 degrees C). Line 2 baking sheets with aluminum foil and grease the foil.

Step 2

Beat egg whites with cream of tartar and salt in a bowl with an electric mixer until egg whites are foamy. Gradually beat in sugar, a few tablespoons at a time, beating until the sugar dissolves in the meringue before adding more. Continue beating until the meringue is glossy and forms a sharp peak when beaters are lifted straight up out of the bowl; beat in vanilla extract. Spoon the meringue into a pastry bag fitted with a small tip.

Step 3

Pipe meringue into small bone shapes on the prepared aluminum foil. You must pipe all the shapes at once or the meringue will deflate.

Step 4

Place cookie sheets into the preheated oven and bake for 1 hour. No not open oven door or peek during baking. Turn the oven off and let the meringue bones cool in the oven without opening door for 1 hour. Gently and carefully remove cookies from aluminum to prevent broken bones.

Nutrition Facts

Per Serving:

32.1 calories; protein 0.6g 1% DV; carbohydrates 7.5g 2% DV; fatg; cholesterolmg; sodium 9.3mg.

Chocolate Spiders

Prep: 5 mins **Cook:** 25 mins **Total:** 30 mins **Servings:** 20 **Yield:** 20 spiders

Ingredients

- 1 pound chocolate confectioners' coating

- 1 (8.5 ounce) package chow mein noodles

Directions

Step 1

Chop the chocolate confectioners' coating and place into a heatproof bowl over simmering water. Cook, stirring occasionally until melted and smooth. Remove from heat and stir in the chow mein noodles so they are evenly distributed. Spoon out to desired size onto waxed paper. Let cool completely before storing or serving.

Nutrition Facts

Per Serving:

172.1 calories; protein 2.8g 6% DV; carbohydrates 17.6g 6% DV; fat 12.7g 20% DV; cholesterolmg; sodium 53.7mg 2% DV.

Peanut Butter Spider Cookies

Prep: 45 mins **Cook:** 10 mins **Total:** 55 mins **Servings:** 48 **Yield:** 48 cookies

Ingredients

- ½ cup shortening
- ½ cup peanut butter
- ½ cup packed brown sugar
- ½ cup white sugar
- 1 egg, beaten
- 2 tablespoons milk
- 1 teaspoon vanilla extract
- 1 ¾ cups all-purpose flour
- 1 teaspoon baking soda
- ½ teaspoon salt
- ¼ cup white sugar for rolling
- 24 piece (blank)s chocolate candy spheres with smooth chocolate filling (such as Lindt Lindor Truffles), refrigerated until cold
- 48 eaches decorative candy eyeballs
- ½ cup prepared chocolate frosting

Directions

Step 1

Preheat oven to 375 degrees F (190 degrees C). Line baking sheets with baking parchment.

Step 2

Beat shortening, peanut butter, brown sugar, and 1/2 cup white sugar together with an electric mixer in a large bowl until smooth. Beat egg into the creamy mixture until fully incorporated. Stir milk and vanilla extract into the mixture until smooth.

Step 3

Mix flour, baking soda, and salt together in a small bowl; add to the wet mixture in the large bowl and stir until completely incorporated into a dough. Divide and shape dough into 48 balls.

Step 4

Spread 1/4 cup white sugar into a wide, shallow bowl. Roll dough balls in sugar to coat and arrange about 2 inches apart onto prepared baking sheets.

Step 5

Bake in preheated oven until golden brown, 10 to 12 minutes. Remove cookies from oven and quickly press a dimple into the middle of each cookie using the blunt end of a wooden spoon. Cool cookies on sheets for 10 minutes before transferring to a wire cooling rack to cool completely.

Step 6

Cut each chocolate sphere into two hemispheres. Put one piece atop each cookie with the rounded side facing upwards.

Step 7

Spoon frosting into a pastry bag with a small round tip or a plastic freezer bag with one end snipped off. Dab a small amount of frosting onto the back of each candy eyeball and stick two onto each chocolate candy to resemble eyes. Then pipe frosting in four thin lines, starting at the base of the candy, on each side atop the cookie to resemble spider legs.

Step 8

Let frosting harden at room temperature, about 30 minutes. Store cookies in an airtight container.

Nutrition Facts

Per Serving:

117.2 calories; protein 1.7g 3% DV; carbohydrates 14.4g 5% DV; fat 6.3g 10% DV; cholesterol 7mg 2% DV; sodium 78mg 3% DV.

Owl Cookies

Servings: 36 **Yield:** 72 cookies

Ingredients

- 1 ¼ cups candy-coated milk chocolate pieces
- 2 tablespoons milk
- 24 ounces dry sugar cookie mix
- 1 cup cashew halves

Directions

Step 1

In a small saucepan combine 3/4 cup of the candies and milk. Melt over low heat, stirring until smooth. Remove from heat.

Step 2

Prepare cookie mixes according to package directions. Stir melted chocolate into half the dough. Form chocolate dough into two 12-inch long rolls about 1 inch in diameter. Wrap in wax paper or foil. Chill until firm, about 2 hours.

Step 3

Divide plain dough in half. On a well-floured surface, roll each plain half out to a 12 x 6 inch rectangle. Place a chocolate roll on long edge. Roll up, pressing doughs lightly together so plain dough encases chocolate roll. Repeat with remaining dough.

Step 4

Wrap each roll in wax paper or foil. Chill about 2 hours until firm. Preheat oven to 375 F (190 C).

Step 5

Cut each roll into 1/4 inch slices. Place 2 slices so they are touching on greased baking sheet. In the center of each chocolate circle, place one of the remaining candies for eye. Where the slices touch, place a cashew to form nose.

Step 6

Bake until the plain cookie is lightly browned, 8 to 10 minutes. Cool cookies on baking sheets 2 to 3 minutes. Remove and cool on wire racks.

Nutrition Facts

Per Serving:

150.8 calories; protein 1.9g 4% DV; carbohydrates 19.9g 6% DV; fat 7.2g 11% DV; cholesterol 7.1mg 2% DV; sodium 103.8mg 4% DV.

Halloween Ghost Cookies

Prep: 45 mins **Cook:** 6 mins **Additional:** 2 hrs 15 mins **Total:** 3 hrs 6 mins **Servings:** 90 **Yield:** 90 cookies

Ingredients

- 1 cup butter
- 1 ½ cups confectioners' sugar
- 1 egg
- 1 teaspoon vanilla extract

- 2 ½ cups all-purpose flour
- 1 teaspoon baking soda
- 1 teaspoon cream of tartar
- ¼ teaspoon salt

- Icing:
- 1 cup confectioners' sugar
- 2 teaspoons milk, plus more if needed
- 2 teaspoons light corn syrup, or more as needed
- ¼ teaspoon vanilla extract
- 1 (12 ounce) package miniature semisweet chocolate chips

Directions

Step 1

Beat butter in a bowl with an electric mixer until creamy. Add 1 1/2 cups confectioners' sugar gradually, beating until light and fluffy. Beat in egg and 1 teaspoon vanilla extract.

Step 2

Combine flour, baking soda, cream of tartar, and salt in a second bowl. Add flour mixture to the creamed butter mixture and mix to combine. Wrap in plastic wrap and chill in the refrigerator for at least 1 hour.

Step 3

Preheat oven to 400 degrees F (200 degrees C).

Step 4

Dust a work surface with flour and roll out dough into a thin circle. Cut out tulip shapes; if your tulip cookie cutter has a stem, cut the stem off with a knife, so you have a stemless tulip shape. Arrange cut-out cookies on ungreased baking sheets.

Step 5

Bake in the preheated oven until lightly browned, 6 to 8 minutes. Remove from baking sheets carefully and transfer to wire racks. Cool completely, about 15 minutes.

Step 6

Stir 1 cup confectioners' sugar and milk together in a small bowl until smooth. Beat in corn syrup and 1/4 teaspoon vanilla extract until icing is smooth and glossy. Add more corn syrup if icing is too thick.

Step 7

Spoon icing into a piping bag with a small plain tip. Pipe icing around the edge of each cookie to create a border. Fill in the middle completely with icing. Stick 2 chocolate chip cookies into the wet icing for the eyes. Let cookies stand until icing dries, about 1 hour.

Nutrition Facts

Per Serving:

63.5 calories; protein 0.6g 1% DV; carbohydrates 8.6g 3% DV; fat 3.3g 5% DV; cholesterol 7.5mg 3% DV; sodium 36.4mg 2% DV.

Meringue Bones and Ghosts

Prep: 15 mins **Cook:** 1 hr **Additional:** 1 hr **Total:** 2 hrs 15 mins **Servings:** 6 **Yield:** 24 bones and ghosts

Ingredients

- 2 large egg whites large egg whites
- 2 drops fresh lemon juice, or more to taste
- 7 tablespoons white sugar, or more to taste
- 2 eaches chocolate chips, melted, or as needed

Directions

Step 1

Preheat oven to 225 degrees F (110 degrees C). Line 2 baking sheets with silicone baking mats.

Step 2

Whisk eggs whites and lemon juice together in a bowl until thick, white, and foamy. Add sugar a spoonful at a time, whisking constantly, until meringue is shiny, thick, and holds its shape.

Step 3

Transfer meringue to a piping bag. Pipe 12 bone shapes onto a prepared baking sheet. Pipe 12 puffs to resemble ghosts onto the remaining baking sheet.

Step 4

Bake in the preheated oven until dried and firm, about 1 hour. Turn off the oven, close the door, and cool until completely dried, about 1 hour more.

Step 5

Dip the tip of a toothpick into melted chocolate and dot chocolate "eyes" on each of the ghosts.

Nutrition Facts

Per Serving:

87.4 calories; protein 1.4g 3% DV; carbohydrates 18.1g 6% DV; fat 1.6g 3% DV; cholesterolmg; sodium 19.1mg 1% DV.

Oreo Devils

Prep: 30 mins **Cook:** 5 mins **Additional:** 1 hr **Total:** 1 hr 35 mins **Servings:** 36 **Yield:** 36 servings

Ingredients

- 2 ounces red fondant
- 1 (12 ounce) package red confectioner's coating (such as Wilton Candy Melts)
- 1 (14 ounce) package chocolate sandwich cookies (such as Oreo)
- 72 eaches small candy eyeballs

Directions

Step 1

Shape red fondant into 72 little horns relative to the size of the cookies. Line 2 baking sheets with parchment paper.

Step 2

Place red confectioner's coating in the top of a double boiler over simmering water. Stir constantly, scraping down the sides with a rubber spatula to avoid scorching, until melted, about 5 minutes. Remove from heat.

Step 3

Use a spoon to cover the top and sides of each cookie with melted red coating. Place on the prepared baking sheet. Stick 2 small devil horns near the top and add 2 candy eyeballs. Let stand until dry, about 1 hour.

Nutrition Facts

Per Serving:

118.1 calories; protein 1.2g 2% DV; carbohydrates 16.3g 5% DV; fat 5.6g 9% DV; cholesterol 2mg 1% DV; sodium 62mg 3% DV.

Royal Icing I

Servings: 32 **Yield:** 2 cups

Ingredients

- 4 large egg whites egg whites
- 4 cups sifted confectioners' sugar
- 1 teaspoon lemon extract

Directions

Step 1

Beat egg whites in a clean, large bowl with mixer at high speed until foamy (use only grade A clean, uncracked eggs). Gradually add sugar and lemon extract. Beat at high speed until thickened.

Nutrition Facts

Per Serving:

63.3 calories; protein 0.5g 1% DV; carbohydrates 15.6g 5% DV; fatg; cholesterolmg; sodium 7.1mg.

Pumpkin Whoopie Pies

Servings: 18 **Yield:** 3 dozen

Ingredients

- 2 cups packed brown sugar
- 1 cup vegetable oil
- 1 ½ cups solid pack pumpkin puree
- 2 large eggs eggs
- 3 cups all-purpose flour
- 1 teaspoon salt
- 1 teaspoon baking powder
- 1 teaspoon baking soda
- 1 teaspoon vanilla extract
- 1 ½ tablespoons ground cinnamon
- ½ tablespoon ground ginger
- ½ tablespoon ground cloves
- 1 egg white
- 2 tablespoons milk
- 1 teaspoon vanilla extract
- 2 cups confectioners' sugar
- ¾ cup shortening

Directions

Step 1

Preheat oven to 350 degrees F (175 degrees C). Lightly grease baking sheets.

Step 2

Combine the oil and brown sugar. Mix in the pumpkin and eggs, beating well. Add the flour, salt, baking powder, baking soda, 1 teaspoon vanilla, cinnamon, ginger and cloves. Mix well.

Step 3

Drop dough by heaping teaspoons onto the prepared baking sheets. Bake at 350 degrees F (175 degrees C) for 10 to 12 minutes. Let cookies cool then make sandwiches from two cookies filled with Whoopie Pie Filling.

Step 4

To Make Whoopie Pie Filling: Beat egg white and mix with the milk, 1 teaspoon vanilla and 1 cup of the confectioners' sugar. Mix well then beat in the shortening and the remaining cup of confectioners' sugar. Beat until light and fluffy.

Nutrition Facts

Per Serving:

424.8 calories; protein 3.4g 7% DV; carbohydrates 55.8g 18% DV; fat 21.7g 33% DV; cholesterol 20.8mg 7% DV; sodium 294.9mg 12% DV.

Chocolate Cut Out Cookies

Servings: 36 **Yield:** 6 dozen

Ingredients

- 1 cup butter
- 2 cups white sugar
- 3 large eggs eggs
- 3 teaspoons vanilla extract
- 3 cups all-purpose flour
- 1 teaspoon baking powder
- 10 tablespoons unsweetened cocoa powder

Directions

Step 1

Cream butter or margarine and sugar until light and fluffy; add eggs, one at a time, beating well. Mix in the vanilla. Combine flour, cocoa powder and baking powder; add and mix well. Wrap dough in waxed paper and chill for 2 hours.

Step 2

Preheat oven to 350 degrees F (175 degrees C).

Step 3

Divide dough in half. Roll out each half to 1/4 inch thick. Cut with desired shaped cookie cutters. Place on lightly greased cookie sheets and bake for 10-12 minutes.

Nutrition Facts

Per Serving:

136.5 calories; protein 1.9g 4% DV; carbohydrates 20g 7% DV; fat 5.8g 9% DV; cholesterol 29.1mg 10% DV; sodium 56.2mg 2% DV.

Pumpkin Cookies with Penuche Frosting

Prep: 15 mins **Cook:** 12 mins **Additional:** 18 mins **Total:** 45 mins **Servings:** 48 **Yield:** 4 dozen

Ingredients

- 1 cup shortening
- ½ cup packed brown sugar

- ½ cup white sugar
- 1 cup pumpkin puree
- 1 egg
- 1 teaspoon vanilla extract
- 2 cups all-purpose flour
- 1 teaspoon baking soda
- 1 teaspoon baking powder
- 1 teaspoon ground cinnamon
- ½ teaspoon salt
- 1 cup chopped walnuts
- 3 tablespoons butter
- ½ cup packed brown sugar
- ¼ cup milk
- 2 cups confectioners' sugar

Directions

Step 1

Preheat the oven to 350 degrees F (175 degrees C). Grease cookie sheets.

Step 2

In a large bowl, cream together shortening, 1/2 cup brown sugar, and white sugar. Mix in pumpkin, egg, and vanilla. Sift together flour, baking soda, baking powder, cinnamon, and salt; mix into the creamed mixture. Stir in walnuts. Drop dough by heaping spoonfuls onto the prepared baking sheets.

Step 3

Bake for 10 to 12 minutes in the preheated oven. Cool on wire racks.

Step 4

In a small saucepan over medium heat, combine the 3 tablespoons butter and 1/2 cup brown sugar. Bring to a boil; cook and stir for 1 minute, or until slightly thickened. Cool slightly, then stir in the milk, and beat until smooth. Gradually stir in 2 cups confectioners' sugar until frosting has reached desired consistency. Spread on cooled cookies.

Nutrition Facts

Per Serving:

128.2 calories; protein 1.2g 2% DV; carbohydrates 16.4g 5% DV; fat 6.8g 10% DV; cholesterol 5.9mg 2% DV; sodium 81.5mg 3% DV.

Pumpkin Shortbread Bars

Prep: 25 mins **Cook:** 35 mins **Additional:** 1 hr **Total:** 2 hrs **Servings:** 12 **Yield:** 12 bars

Ingredients

- ½ cup softened butter
- ⅓ cup white sugar
- ¼ teaspoon vanilla extract
- 1 cup all-purpose flour
- ⅓ cup all-purpose flour
- ½ teaspoon baking powder

- ¼ teaspoon salt
- 2 large eggs eggs
- 1 cup firmly packed brown sugar
- 1 cup canned solid pack pumpkin
- 1 teaspoon vanilla extract
- ½ cup chopped pecans
- 1 cup all-purpose flour
- ⅓ cup white sugar
- ¼ cup cold butter

Directions

Step 1

Preheat an oven to 400 degrees F (200 degrees C).

Step 2

Beat 1/2 cup butter, 1/3 cup sugar, and 1/4 teaspoon of vanilla extract together until blended. Mix in 1 cup flour until no longer dry. Press into a 9x13-inch baking dish.

Step 3

Bake in the preheated oven for 10 minutes. Remove and allow to cool for a few minutes. Reduce the oven to 350 degrees F (175 degrees C).

Step 4

Whisk together 1/3 cup flour, the baking powder, and salt together in a bowl; set aside. Beat the eggs, brown sugar, pumpkin, 1 teaspoon vanilla extract, and the pecans together in a bowl until the pumpkin is smooth. Stir in the flour mixture until just incorporated and spread the batter over the parbaked crust.

Step 5

Place 1 cup flour, 1/3 cup sugar, and 1/4 cup of cold butter into a bowl. Press the butter into the flour using a pastry blender or fork until no pieces of butter remain and the mixture resembles coarse crumbs. Sprinkle evenly over the pumpkin batter.

Step 6

Bake in the preheated oven until a toothpick inserted into the center comes out clean, 25 to 30 minutes. Cool completely in the pan. Cut into bars before serving.

Nutrition Facts

Per Serving:

357.5 calories; protein 4.5g 9% DV; carbohydrates 50.1g 16% DV; fat 16.2g 25% DV; cholesterol 61.5mg 21% DV; sodium 168.7mg 7% DV.

Pumpkin Protein Cookies

Prep: 15 mins **Cook:** 5 mins **Total:** 20 mins **Servings:** 14 **Yield:** 14 cookies

Ingredients

- ¾ cup SPLENDA Granular
- 1 cup rolled oats
- 1 cup whole wheat flour
- ½ cup soy flour
- 1 ¾ teaspoons baking soda
- ½ teaspoon baking powder
- ½ teaspoon salt
- 2 teaspoons ground cinnamon
- 1 teaspoon ground nutmeg
- ½ cup pumpkin puree
- 1 tablespoon canola oil
- 2 teaspoons water
- 2 large egg whites egg whites
- 1 teaspoon molasses
- 1 tablespoon flax seeds

Directions

Step 1

Preheat oven to 350 degrees F (175 degrees C).

Step 2

In a large bowl, whisk together Splenda, oats, wheat flour, soy flour, baking soda, baking powder, salt, cinnamon, and nutmeg. Stir in pumpkin, canola oil, water, egg whites, and molasses. Stir in flax seeds, if desired. Roll into 14 large balls, and flatten on a baking sheet.

Step 3

Bake for 5 minutes in preheated oven. DO NOT OVERBAKE: the cookies will come out really dry if overbaked.

Nutrition Facts

Per Serving:

84.8 calories; protein 4.2g 8% DV; carbohydrates 13.1g 4% DV; fat 2.2g 3% DV; cholesterolmg; sodium 284.1mg 11% DV.

White Chocolate Pumpkin Cookies

Servings: 18 **Yield:** 3 dozen

Ingredients

- 2 ¼ cups all-purpose flour
- 1 teaspoon pumpkin pie spice
- ½ teaspoon baking soda
- 1 cup unsalted butter

- 1 ½ cups packed brown sugar
- 1 cup solid pack pumpkin puree
- 2 large eggs eggs
- 1 tablespoon vanilla extract
- 2 cups white chocolate chips
- 1 cup chopped pecans

Directions

Step 1

In a small bowl, whisk together the flour, pumpkin pie spice and baking soda.

Step 2

In a medium bowl, with an electric mixer, cream butter and sugar. Beat in pumpkin pie puree. Beat in the eggs and vanilla. Beat in the flour mixture until just combined. Stir in the white chocolate and pecans.

Step 3

Drop dough by rounded tablespoon 2 inches apart on an ungreased cookie sheet. Bake at 300 degrees F (150 degrees C) for 20-22 minutes until just set.

Nutrition Facts

Per Serving:

386.5 calories; protein 4.6g 9% DV; carbohydrates 43.3g 14% DV; fat 22.4g 34% DV; cholesterol 52mg 17% DV; sodium 103.6mg 4% DV.

Almond Joy Cookies

Prep: 20 mins **Cook:** 8 mins **Additional:** 5 mins **Total:** 33 mins **Servings:** 36 **Yield:** 3 dozen cookies

Ingredients

- 4 ½ cups all-purpose flour
- 2 teaspoons baking soda
- 1 teaspoon salt
- 1 ½ cups white sugar
- 1 ½ cups brown sugar
- 1 ripe banana
- 4 large eggs eggs
- 1 tablespoon vanilla extract
- 5 cups chocolate chips
- 2 cups sweetened flaked coconut
- 2 cups chopped almonds

Directions

Step 1

Preheat oven to 375 degrees F (190 degrees C). Lightly grease baking sheets.

Step 2

Combine flour, baking soda, and salt in a bowl.

Step 3

Beat white sugar, brown sugar, and banana together in a separate bowl until smooth and creamy; beat in eggs, 1 at a time, until well mixed. Stir in vanilla extract.

Step 4

Stir banana mixture into flour mixture until batter is well mixed; fold in chocolate chips, coconut, and almonds. Drop batter by rounded spoonfuls onto the prepared baking sheets.

Step 5

Bake in the preheated oven until edges of cookies are beginning to crisp, 8 to 10 minutes. Cool cookies on baking sheet for 5 minutes before transferring to a wire rack to cool completely.

Nutrition Facts

Per Serving:

285 calories; protein 4.6g 9% DV; carbohydrates 44.9g 15% DV; fat 11.5g 18% DV; cholesterol 20.7mg 7% DV; sodium 158.7mg 6% DV.

Peanut Blossoms II

Prep: 30 mins **Cook:** 12 mins **Additional:** 48 mins **Total:** 1 hr 30 mins **Servings:** 84 **Yield:** 7 dozen

Ingredients

- 1 cup shortening
- 1 cup peanut butter
- 1 cup packed brown sugar
- 1 cup white sugar
- 2 large eggs eggs
- ¼ cup milk
- 2 teaspoons vanilla extract
- 3 ½ cups all-purpose flour
- 2 teaspoons baking soda
- 1 teaspoon salt
- ½ cup white sugar for decoration
- 2 (9 ounce) bags milk chocolate candy kisses, unwrapped

Directions

Step 1

Preheat oven to 375 degrees F (190 degrees C). Grease cookie sheets.

Step 2

In a large bowl, cream together the shortening, peanut butter, brown sugar, and 1 cup white sugar until smooth. Beat in the eggs one at a time, and stir in the milk and vanilla. Combine the flour, baking soda, and salt; stir into the peanut butter mixture until well blended. Shape tablespoonfuls of dough into balls, and roll in remaining white sugar. Place cookies 2 inches apart on the prepared cookie sheets.

Step 3

Bake for 10 to12 minutes in the preheated oven. Remove from oven, and immediately press a chocolate kiss into each cookie. Allow to cool completely; the kiss will harden as it cools.

Nutrition Facts

Per Serving:

115.5 calories; protein 1.9g 4% DV; carbohydrates 14.3g 5% DV; fat 6g 9% DV; cholesterol 5.8mg 2% DV; sodium 79.5mg 3% DV.

Royal Icing II

Prep: 15 mins **Total:** 15 mins **Servings:** 48 **Yield:** 3 cups

Ingredients

- 3 tablespoons meringue powder
- 4 cups sifted confectioners' sugar
- 6 tablespoons water

Directions

Step 1

Beat all ingredients at low speed for 7 to 10 minutes, or until icing forms peaks. Tip: Keep icing covered with a wet kitchen towel at all times. Icing can dry out quickly.

Nutrition Facts

Per Serving:

43.4 calories; protein 0.2g; carbohydrates 10.8g 4% DV; fatg; cholesterolmg; sodium 2.7mg.

Snickers Brownies

Prep: 15 mins **Cook:** 30 mins **Additional:** 30 mins **Total:** 1 hr 15 mins **Servings:** 12 **Yield:** 12 servings

Ingredients

- 1 ½ cups white sugar
- ¾ cup all-purpose flour
- ½ cup unsweetened cocoa powder
- ½ teaspoon salt
- ¼ teaspoon baking powder
- ¾ cup butter, melted
- 3 large eggs eggs
- 1 teaspoon vanilla extract
- 2 cups chocolate-coated caramel-peanut nougat candy (such as Snickers), chopped, divided

Directions

Step 1

Preheat the oven to 350 degrees F (175 degrees C). Grease a 9-inch square baking pan.

Step 2

Mix sugar, flour, cocoa powder, salt, and baking powder together in a mixing bowl.

Step 3

Mix butter, eggs, and vanilla extract together in a separate bowl; add butter mixture to the bowl with the flour mixture and stir batter until well mixed.

Step 4

Pour 1/2 the batter into the prepared baking pan. Top with 1/2 the candy bar pieces. Spread remaining batter on top, covering candy completely.

Step 5

Bake in the preheated oven until edges are brown and center is set, about 30 minutes.

Step 6

Remove brownies from the oven and spread remaining candy bar pieces on top, lightly pressing them in while the brownies are still hot. Let brownies cool completely before serving, about 30 minutes.

Nutrition Facts

Per Serving:

387.1 calories; protein 5.3g 11% DV; carbohydrates 50g 16% DV; fat 20g 31% DV; cholesterol 80.6mg 27% DV; sodium 276.1mg 11% DV.

Paul's Pumpkin Bars

Prep: 15 mins **Cook:** 30 mins **Total:** 45 mins **Servings:** 24 **Yield:** 2 dozen

Ingredients

- 4 large eggs eggs
- 1 ⅔ cups white sugar
- 1 cup vegetable oil
- 1 (15 ounce) can pumpkin purée
- 2 cups all-purpose flour
- 2 teaspoons baking powder
- 1 teaspoon baking soda
- 2 teaspoons ground cinnamon
- 1 teaspoon salt
- 1 (3 ounce) package cream cheese, softened
- ½ cup butter, softened
- 1 teaspoon vanilla extract

- 2 cups sifted confectioners' sugar

Directions

Step 1

Preheat oven to 350 degrees F (175 degrees C).

Step 2

In a medium bowl, mix the eggs, sugar, oil, and pumpkin with an electric mixer until light and fluffy. Sift together the flour, baking powder, baking soda, cinnamon and salt. Stir into the pumpkin mixture until thoroughly combined.

Step 3

Spread the batter evenly into an ungreased 10x15 inch jellyroll pan. Bake for 25 to 30 minutes in preheated oven. Cool before frosting.

Step 4

To make the frosting, cream together the cream cheese and butter. Stir in vanilla. Add confectioners' sugar a little at a time, beating until mixture is smooth. Spread evenly on top of the cooled bars. Cut into squares.

Nutrition Facts

Per Serving:

278.8 calories; protein 2.6g 5% DV; carbohydrates 34.1g 11% DV; fat 15.2g 23% DV; cholesterol 45.1mg 15% DV; sodium 282.5mg 11% DV.

Pumpkin Chocolate Chip Cookies III

Servings: 24 **Yield:** 2 dozen

Ingredients

- 1 cup canned pumpkin
- 1 cup white sugar
- ½ cup vegetable oil
- 1 egg
- 2 cups all-purpose flour
- 2 teaspoons baking powder
- 2 teaspoons ground cinnamon
- ½ teaspoon salt
- 1 teaspoon baking soda
- 1 teaspoon milk
- 1 tablespoon vanilla extract
- 2 cups semisweet chocolate chips
- ½ cup chopped walnuts

Directions

Step 1

Combine pumpkin, sugar, vegetable oil, and egg. In a separate bowl, stir together flour, baking powder, ground cinnamon, and salt. Dissolve the baking soda with the milk and stir in. Add flour mixture to pumpkin mixture and mix well.

Step 2

Add vanilla, chocolate chips and nuts.

Step 3

Drop by spoonful on greased cookie sheet and bake at 350 degrees F (175 degrees C) for approximately 10 minutes or until lightly brown and firm.

Nutrition Facts

Per Serving:

202.4 calories; protein 2.4g 5% DV; carbohydrates 26.6g 9% DV; fat 10.7g 17% DV; cholesterol 7.8mg 3% DV; sodium 170.9mg 7% DV.

Pumpkin Oatmeal Chocolate Chip Cookies

Prep: 15 mins **Cook:** 10 mins **Total:** 25 mins **Servings:** 72 **Yield:** 6 dozen cookies

Ingredients

- 1 ½ cups butter, softened
- 2 cups packed brown sugar
- 1 cup white sugar
- 1 (15 ounce) can pumpkin puree
- 1 egg
- 1 teaspoon vanilla extract
- 4 cups all-purpose flour
- 2 cups quick-cooking oats
- 2 teaspoons ground cinnamon
- 2 teaspoons baking soda
- 1 teaspoon baking powder
- 1 teaspoon salt
- 2 cups miniature chocolate chips

Directions

Step 1

Preheat oven to 375 degrees F (190 degrees C).

Step 2

Beat butter, brown sugar, and white sugar together in a bowl until creamy. Add pumpkin, egg, and vanilla extract; beat until smooth.

Step 3

Mix flour, oats, cinnamon, baking soda, baking powder, and salt in a separate bowl; stir into creamed butter until combined. Fold chocolate chips into batter. Drop 1 to 2 tablespoons batter for each cookie onto a baking sheet.

Step 4

Bake in the preheated oven until the edges of each cookie are lightly browned, 10 to 12 minutes.

Nutrition Facts

Per Serving:

128.1 calories; protein 1.4g 3% DV; carbohydrates 19.2g 6% DV; fat 5.6g 9% DV; cholesterol 12.8mg 4% DV; sodium 119mg 5% DV.

Pumpkin Spice Cookie

Prep: 15 mins **Cook:** 20 mins **Total:** 35 mins **Servings:** 24 **Yield:** 2 dozen cookies

Ingredients

- 1 (18.25 ounce) package spice cake mix
- 1 (15 ounce) can solid pack pumpkin

Directions

Step 1

Preheat oven to 350 degrees F (175 degrees C). Grease cookie sheets.

Step 2

In a large bowl, stir together the cake mix and pumpkin until well blended. Drop by rounded spoonfuls onto the prepared cookie sheet.

Step 3

Bake for 18 to 20 minutes in the preheated oven. Allow cookies to cool on baking sheet for 5 minutes before removing to a wire rack to cool completely.

Nutrition Facts

Per Serving:

98 calories; protein 1.5g 3% DV; carbohydrates 17.2g 6% DV; fat 2.7g 4% DV; cholesterolmg; sodium 187.8mg 8% DV.

Pumpkin Pie Bars

Prep: 15 mins **Cook:** 45 mins **Additional:** 1 hr **Total:** 2 hrs **Servings:** 24 **Yield:** 1 9x13-inch pan

Ingredients

- 1 (18.25 ounce) package yellow cake mix
- ½ cup melted butter
- 3 large eggs eggs
- 3 cups pumpkin pie filling
- ⅔ cup milk
- ¼ cup white sugar
- 1 teaspoon ground cinnamon
- ¼ cup butter

Directions

Step 1

Preheat oven to 350 degrees F (190 degrees C). Grease the bottom of a 9x13 inch pan.

Step 2

Pour one cup of yellow cake mix into a medium size mixing bowl; set aside.

Step 3

Combine remaining cake mix, 1/2 cup melted butter and 1 egg; mix well. Press into the baking pan.

Step 4

Combine pumpkin pie filling, 2 eggs and milk in a medium size mixing bowl; mix until smooth. Pour evenly over the crust in the 9x13 inch pan.

Step 5

Pour the sugar and cinnamon into the mixing bowl containing the 1 cup of yellow cake mix. Cut in the butter until the mixture looks crumbly. Sprinkle this mixture over the pumpkin filling.

Step 6

Bake for 45 to 50 minutes or until a knife inserted into the bars come out clean. Let cool before slicing.

Nutrition Facts

Per Serving:

188.3 calories; protein 2.4g 5% DV; carbohydrates 28.3g 9% DV; fat 7.8g 12% DV; cholesterol 36.2mg 12% DV; sodium 262.9mg 11% DV.

Pumpkin Cookies with Cream Cheese Frosting (The World's Best!)

Prep: 30 mins **Cook:** 10 mins **Additional:** 30 mins **Total:** 1 hr 10 mins **Servings:** 36 **Yield:** 3 dozen cookies

Ingredients

- 2 cups all-purpose flour
- 1 teaspoon baking powder
- 1 teaspoon ground cinnamon
- ½ teaspoon baking soda
- ½ teaspoon ground nutmeg
- ½ teaspoon ground ginger
- 1 cup butter
- ¾ cup white sugar
- ¾ cup brown sugar
- 2 teaspoons vanilla extract
- 1 egg
- 1 (15 ounce) can pumpkin puree
- 1 (3 ounce) package cream cheese, softened
- ¼ cup butter, softened
- 1 teaspoon vanilla extract
- 2 cups confectioners' sugar

Directions

Step 1

Preheat oven to 350 degrees F (175 degrees C). Lightly grease baking sheets.

Step 2

Whisk flour, baking powder, cinnamon, baking soda, nutmeg, and ginger together in a bowl. Beat 1 cup butter, white sugar, brown sugar, 2 teaspoons vanilla extract, and egg with an electric mixer in a separate large bowl, beating until mixture is smooth. Beat in pumpkin puree. Gradually stir dry ingredients into pumpkin mixture. Batter will be moist.

Step 3

Spoon batter by teaspoonfuls about 2 inches apart onto prepared baking sheets.

Step 4

Bake in the preheated oven until cookies are lightly browned, 10 to 12 minutes. Let cookies cool for about 5 minutes on sheets before removing to finish cooling on waxed paper.

Step 5

Beat cream cheese, 1/4 cup butter, and 1 teaspoon vanilla extract in a bowl with an electric mixer until soft and creamy. Beat in confectioners' sugar, about 1/2 cup at a time, until frosting is smooth and spreadable. Frost cooled cookies with cream cheese frosting.

Nutrition Facts

Per Serving:

152.3 calories; protein 1.3g 3% DV; carbohydrates 20.6g 7% DV; fat 7.5g 12% DV; cholesterol 24.7mg 8% DV; sodium 115mg 5% DV.

Pumpkin Chocolate Chip Cookies I

Prep: 15 mins **Cook:** 15 mins **Additional:** 15 mins **Total:** 45 mins **Servings:** 48 **Yield:** 4 dozen

Ingredients

- ½ cup shortening
- 1 ½ cups white sugar
- 1 egg
- 1 cup canned pumpkin
- 1 teaspoon vanilla extract
- 2 ½ cups all-purpose flour
- 1 teaspoon baking powder
- 1 teaspoon baking soda
- 1 teaspoon salt
- 1 teaspoon ground nutmeg
- 1 teaspoon ground cinnamon
- ½ cup chopped walnuts
- 1 cup semisweet chocolate chips

Directions

Step 1

Preheat oven to 350 degrees F (175 degrees C). Grease cookie sheets.

Step 2

In a large bowl, cream together the shortening and sugar until light and fluffy. Beat in the egg, then stir in the pumpkin and vanilla. Combine the flour, baking powder, baking soda, salt, nutmeg, and cinnamon; gradually mix into the creamed mixture. Stir in the walnuts and chocolate chips. Drop dough by teaspoonfuls onto the prepared cookie sheets.

Step 3

Bake for 15 minutes in the preheated oven, or until light brown. Cool on wire racks.

Nutrition Facts

Per Serving:

95.5 calories; protein 1.2g 2% DV; carbohydrates 14.1g 5% DV; fat 4.2g 6% DV; cholesterol 3.9mg 1% DV; sodium 99.1mg 4% DV.

Extra Easy Pumpkin Cookies

Prep: 15 mins **Cook:** 8 mins **Total:** 23 mins **Servings:** 24 **Yield:** 2 dozen cookies

Ingredients

- 1 (14 ounce) can 100% pure pumpkin
- 2 large eggs eggs
- ½ cup applesauce
- ½ teaspoon vanilla extract
- 1 (18.25 ounce) package spice cake mix
- 1 teaspoon cinnamon
- ½ teaspoon ground nutmeg
- ¼ teaspoon ground cloves

Directions

Step 1

Preheat oven to 350 degrees F (175 degrees C). Lightly grease two baking sheets.

Step 2

Beat the pumpkin, eggs, applesauce, and vanilla together in a large mixing bowl. Stir in the cake mix, cinnamon, nutmeg, and cloves until well blended and creamy. Drop by spoonfuls on prepared baking sheets.

Step 3

Bake in preheated oven until tops are firm when lightly touched, 8 to 10 minutes. Cool on racks.

Nutrition Facts

Per Serving:

106.6 calories; protein 2g 4% DV; carbohydrates 17.8g 6% DV; fat 3.2g 5% DV; cholesterol 15.5mg 5% DV; sodium 190.9mg 8% DV.

Chocolate Chip Pumpkin Cookies

Prep: 10 mins **Cook:** 15 mins **Additional:** 10 mins **Total:** 35 mins **Servings:** 84 **Yield:** 7 dozen

Ingredients

- 1 cup shortening
- 2 cups white sugar
- 2 large eggs eggs
- 2 teaspoons vanilla extract
- 1 (15 ounce) can pumpkin puree
- 4 cups all-purpose flour
- 1 ½ teaspoons baking soda
- 1 ½ teaspoons baking powder
- 1 teaspoon salt
- 1 teaspoon ground cinnamon
- 1 pinch ground nutmeg
- 1 cup semisweet chocolate chips
- 1 cup chopped walnuts

Directions

Step 1

Preheat the oven to 375 degrees F (190 degrees C). Grease cookie sheets.

Step 2

In a large bowl, cream together the shortening and white sugar until smooth. Beat in the eggs one at a time. Stir in the vanilla and pumpkin until well blended. Combine the flour, baking soda, baking powder, salt, cinnamon and nutmeg; stir into the pumpkin mixture. Mix in the chocolate chips. Stir in the walnuts if desired. Drop by teaspoonfuls onto the prepared cookie sheets.

Step 3

Bake for 12 to 15 minutes in the preheated oven, until edges begin to brown. Allow to cool for a few minutes on the baking sheets before removing to wire racks to cool completely.

Nutrition Facts

Per Serving:

84.2 calories; protein 1.1g 2% DV; carbohydrates 11.2g 4% DV; fat 4.1g 6% DV; cholesterol 4.4mg 2% DV; sodium 70.9mg 3% DV.

Root Beer Float Cookies

Prep: 15 mins **Cook:** 8 mins **Total:** 23 mins **Servings:** 24 **Yield:** 24 cookies

Ingredients

- ¾ cup butter
- ¾ cup brown sugar
- ¼ cup white sugar
- 1 (3.5 ounce) package instant vanilla pudding mix
- 2 large eggs eggs
- 1 teaspoon root beer concentrate
- 2 ¼ cups all-purpose flour
- 1 teaspoon baking soda
- 1 cup white chocolate chips, or more to taste

Directions

Step 1

Preheat oven to 350 degrees F (175 degrees C). Grease 2 baking sheets.

Step 2

Beat butter, brown sugar, and white sugar together in a bowl with an electric mixer until creamy; beat in pudding mix. Add eggs and root beer concentrate; stir in flour and baking soda. Fold chocolate chips into the dough.

Step 3

Drop spoonfuls of dough 2 inches apart on the baking sheets.

Step 4

Bake in the preheated oven until golden, 8 to 10 minutes.

Nutrition Facts

Per Serving:

182.1 calories; protein 2.3g 5% DV; carbohydrates 23.5g 8% DV; fat 8.9g 14% DV; cholesterol 32.3mg 11% DV; sodium 167.4mg 7% DV.

Soft Pumpkin Cookies

Servings: 12 **Yield:** 1 dozen

Ingredients

- 1 cup white sugar
- 1 tablespoon butter
- 1 egg, beaten
- 1 teaspoon vanilla extract
- 1 cup pumpkin puree
- ½ cup chopped walnuts
- 2 cups all-purpose flour
- 1 teaspoon baking powder
- ½ teaspoon salt

Directions

Step 1

Preheat oven to 375 degrees F (190 degrees C).

Step 2

Cream together sugar and butter. Add egg, vanilla, pumpkin and walnuts.

Step 3

Stir in flour, baking powder and salt; mix well.

Step 4

Drop by the tablespoon on cookie sheet and bake for 15 minutes.

Nutrition Facts

Per Serving:

192 calories; protein 3.6g 7% DV; carbohydrates 34.4g 11% DV; fat 4.8g 7% DV; cholesterol 18mg 6% DV; sodium 150.9mg 6% DV.

Broiler S'mores

Prep: 5 mins **Cook:** 3 mins **Total:** 8 mins **Servings:** 4 **Yield:** 4 servings

Ingredients

- 4 cracker (2-1/2" square)s graham crackers
- 2 eaches milk chocolate candy bars
- 12 regulars marshmallows

Directions

Step 1

Preheat the oven broiler. Line a small pan with aluminum foil and lightly coat with cooking spray.

Step 2

Break the graham crackers in half and lay 4 of the squares out on a serving plate. Break the candy bars in half and lay one piece on each of the graham crackers on the plate.

Step 3

Arrange the marshmallows in a single layer in the prepared pan.

Step 4

Broil the marshmallows until the tops brown, turn the marshmallows to brown the undersides. Keep a close eye on the marshmallows so they do not burn. They will brown very quickly.

Step 5

Remove the marshmallows from the pan and place three on each of the chocolate squares. Top with the remaining graham cracker halves.

Nutrition Facts

Per Serving:

208.3 calories; protein 1.9g 4% DV; carbohydrates 35.9g 12% DV; fat 7.3g 11% DV; cholesterol 5mg 2% DV; sodium 72.1mg 3% DV.

Pumpkin Cookies V

Servings: 18 **Yield:** 3 dozen

Ingredients

- 2 cups shortening
- 2 cups white sugar
- 2 cups canned pumpkin
- 2 large eggs eggs
- 2 teaspoons baking soda
- 1 ½ teaspoons ground cinnamon
- 1 teaspoon salt
- 4 cups all-purpose flour
- 6 tablespoons butter
- 8 tablespoons milk
- 2 cups confectioners' sugar
- 1 ½ teaspoons vanilla extract
- 1 cup packed brown sugar

Directions

Step 1

Cream shortening, white sugar and pumpkin. Add eggs and mix well. Sift together the baking soda, ground cinnamon, salt and flour. Add to pumpkin mixture and mix well.

Step 2

Drop from spoon to cookie sheet. Bake 10 minutes at 350 degrees F (175 degrees C).

Step 3

To Make Frosting: Cook butter, milk, and brown sugar until dissolved. Cool and add confectioners' sugar and vanilla. Spread over warm cookies.

Nutrition Facts

Per Serving:

542.8 calories; protein 4.2g 8% DV; carbohydrates 71.4g 23% DV; fat 27.7g 43% DV; cholesterol 31.4mg 11% DV; sodium 376.6mg 15% DV.

Peanut Candy Bar Cake

Servings: 24 **Yield:** 1 -9x13 inch cake

Ingredients

- 1 (18.25 ounce) package yellow cake mix
- ⅓ cup butter
- 3 cups miniature marshmallows
- ⅔ cup light corn syrup
- 1 egg
- 2 teaspoons vanilla extract
- 2 cups peanut butter chips
- 2 cups salted peanuts

- 1 ½ cups crisp rice cereal
- ¼ cup butter

Directions

Step 1

Preheat oven to 350 degrees F (175 degrees C).

Step 2

Mix together the cake mix, 1/3 cup butter or margarine and, the egg. Press into the bottom of one 9x13 inch pan and bake at 350 degrees F (175 degrees C) for 12 to 18 minutes. Remove from oven and sprinkle with miniature marshmallows. Return to oven for 1 to 2 minutes or until the marshmallows begin to puff.

Step 3

In a saucepan over medium heat cook corn syrup, 1/4 cup butter of margarine, vanilla, and peanut butter chips until melted. Remove from heat and stir in the puffed rice cereal and salted peanuts. Spoon mixture over top of marshmallow topped cake and spread to cover. Allow to cool before serving.

Nutrition Facts

Per Serving:

373.2 calories; protein 8.6g 17% DV; carbohydrates 43g 14% DV; fat 18.9g 29% DV; cholesterol 20mg 7% DV; sodium 348.8mg 14% DV.

Peanutty Candy Corn Cereal Bars

Prep: 15 mins **Cook:** 5 mins **Additional:** 30 mins **Total:** 50 mins **Servings:** 12 **Yield:** 1 9x13-inch pan

Ingredients

- ¼ cup margarine
- 1 tablespoon peanut butter
- 5 cups miniature marshmallows, divided
- 6 cups honey nut-flavored cereal squares (such as Honey Nut Chex)
- 2 cups candy corn
- ½ cup peanuts

Directions

Step 1

Grease a 9x13-inch baking pan.

Step 2

Cook and stir margarine and peanut butter together in a saucepan over medium heat until smooth, 2 to 3 minutes. Add 4 cups marshmallows to margarine mixture; cook and stir until marshmallows are melted, 2 to 3 minutes. Remove saucepan from heat.

Step 3

Stir cereal squares into marshmallow mixture until fully coated and slightly cooled; fold in candy corn, peanuts, and remaining 1 cup marshmallows. Pour mixture into the prepared baking pan, pressing down in an even layer with buttered hands or a buttered wooden spoon. Cool completely before cutting into squares.

Nutrition Facts

Per Serving:

343.3 calories; protein 3.2g 6% DV; carbohydrates 63.9g 21% DV; fat 7.8g 12% DV; cholesterolmg; sodium 226.3mg 9% DV.

Halloween Finger Cookies

Prep: 30 mins **Cook:** 20 mins **Total:** 50 mins **Servings:** 50 **Yield:** 50 cookies

Ingredients

- 1 cup unsalted butter
- ¾ cup confectioners' sugar
- 1 teaspoon vanilla extract
- ½ teaspoon salt

- 1 ¾ cups all-purpose flour
- 1 cup ground pecans
- 50 almonds almonds

Directions

Step 1

Preheat the oven to 300 degrees F (150 degrees C). Line a baking sheet with parchment paper.

Step 2

Beat butter and sugar together using an electric mixer until fluffy. Blend in vanilla extract and salt. Mix in flour and ground pecans. Shape about 1 tablespoon of dough into a finger, about 3 inches long and 3/4 inch wide. Repeat with remaining dough to form about 50 fingers total.

Step 3

Place fingers 2 inches apart on the prepared baking sheet; they will expand a little while baking. Stick an almond 'nail' onto the end of each finger. Lightly score some 'knuckles' into the centers using a knife.

Step 4

Bake in the preheated oven until set and very lightly browned, about 20 minutes. Let cool.

Nutrition Facts

Per Serving:

74.2 calories; protein 0.9g 2% DV; carbohydrates 5.6g 2% DV; fat 5.5g 9% DV; cholesterol 9.8mg 3% DV; sodium 23.9mg 1% DV.

Spiderweb Brownies

Prep: 15 mins **Cook:** 40 mins **Additional:** 30 mins **Total:** 1 hr 25 mins **Servings:** 16 **Yield:** 16 servings

Ingredients

- 1 (18.25 ounce) package chocolate brownie mix
- 2 (2.1 ounce) bars NESTLE BUTTERFINGER Original, chopped
- 1 (3 ounce) package cream cheese, at room temperature
- ¼ cup granulated sugar
- 2 tablespoons milk

Directions

Step 1

Preheat oven to 350 degrees F. Grease 9- or 10-inch-round baking pan.

Step 2

Prepare brownie batter according to package directions; stir in chopped Butterfinger. Spoon into prepared pan.

Step 3

Beat cream cheese, sugar and milk in small mixer bowl until smooth. Pipe cream cheese mixture into concentric circles over brownie batter. Using wooden pick or tip of knife, pull tip through cream cheese from center to last circle to create a spiderweb effect.

Step 4

Bake for 40 minutes or until wooden pick inserted near center comes out almost clean. Cool completely in pan on wire rack. Cut into wedges using wet knife.

Nutrition Facts

Per Serving:

205.7 calories; protein 2.3g 5% DV; carbohydrates 33.5g 11% DV; fat 8.1g 12% DV; cholesterol 6mg 2% DV; sodium 131.4mg 5% DV.

Halloween Candy Blondies

Prep: 20 mins **Cook:** 30 mins **Additional:** 30 mins **Total:** 1 hr 20 mins **Servings:** 12 **Yield:** 12 blondies

Ingredients

- 1 cup all-purpose flour
- ½ teaspoon baking powder
- ½ cup salted butter, softened
- ½ cup white sugar
- ¼ cup dark brown sugar
- ¼ cup sugar and sucralose blend for baking (such as Natur Bakers Blend)
- 1 large egg
- 1 teaspoon vanilla extract
- ½ cup white chocolate chips
- ¼ cup candy-coated milk chocolate pieces
- ¼ cup candy corn
- 3 tablespoons sliced almonds

Directions

Step 1

Preheat the oven to 350 degrees F (175 degrees C). Lightly butter an 8-inch square baking pan.

Step 2

Whisk flour and baking powder in a small bowl to remove any lumps.

Step 3

Beat butter with white sugar, brown sugar, and sugar blend in a large bowl until well combined. Stir in egg and vanilla extract, beating until smooth. Add flour mixture and blend until just combined, taking care not to overbeat the batter.

Step 4

Gently fold white chocolate chips, milk chocolate pieces, candy corn, and almonds into the batter. Spread batter into the prepared pan.

Step 5

Bake in the preheated oven until a toothpick inserted in the center comes out clean, 30 to 35 minutes. Let cool for at least 30 minutes before cutting into bars.

Nutrition Facts

Per Serving:

269 calories; protein 2.7g 5% DV; carbohydrates 36g 12% DV; fat 12.5g 19% DV; cholesterol 38mg 13% DV; sodium 93.1mg 4% DV.

Pumpkin Cookies with Maple Icing

Prep: 15 mins **Cook:** 15 mins **Additional:** 25 mins **Total:** 55 mins **Servings:** 24 **Yield:** 24 cookies

Ingredients

Cookies:

- 2 cups all-purpose flour
- 1 teaspoon baking powder
- 1 teaspoon baking soda
- ½ teaspoon salt
- 1 teaspoon pumpkin pie spice
- ½ cup shortening
- 1 cup brown sugar
- 1 cup pumpkin puree
- 1 large egg
- 1 teaspoon vanilla extract

Icing:

- ½ cup unsalted butter, at room temperature
- ¼ cup maple syrup
- 2 tablespoons pumpkin puree
- 1 teaspoon pumpkin pie spice
- 1 teaspoon vanilla extract
- 1 (16 ounce) package powdered sugar
- 1 drop orange gel food coloring, or as desired
- 1 tablespoon black sprinkles, or as desired

Directions

Step 1

Preheat the oven to 350 degrees F (175 degrees C). Line 2 baking sheets with parchment paper.

Step 2

Sift flour, baking powder, baking soda, salt, and pumpkin pie spice for cookies together in a large bowl. Set aside.

Step 3

Combine shortening and brown sugar in a second large bowl. Beat using an electric mixer until light and fluffy, about 1 minute. Add pumpkin, egg, and vanilla extract; mix well until combined. Add 1/2 of the flour mixture and mix well. Add remaining flour mixture and mix again.

Step 4

Scoop tablespoonfuls of dough onto the prepared baking sheets, arranging 2 inches apart.

Step 5

Bake in the preheated oven until lightly browned at the edges, about 14 minutes, rotating baking sheets from top to bottom and front to back halfway through baking time.

Step 6

While the cookies bake, combine butter and maple syrup for icing in a medium bowl. Beat using an electric mixer until smooth. Add pumpkin, pumpkin pie spice, and vanilla extract. Mix well. Add powdered sugar and beat until fluffy. Add food coloring and beat until uniform. Set aside.

Step 7

Remove cookies from the oven and let cool on baking sheets for 5 minutes. Transfer cookies to a wire rack to cool completely, 20 to 30 minutes more. Pipe or spread icing onto cooled cookies and decorate with sprinkles as desired.

Nutrition Facts

Per Serving:

224.7 calories; protein 1.5g 3% DV; carbohydrates 36.2g 12% DV; fat 8.6g 13% DV; cholesterol 17.9mg 6% DV; sodium 154.9mg 6% DV.

Crispy Rice Candy Corn Treats

Prep: 5 mins **Cook:** 10 mins **Additional:** 5 mins **Total:** 20 mins **Servings:** 24 **Yield:** 1 15x10-inch pan

Ingredients

- 9 cups miniature marshmallows
- ½ cup butter
- 10 cups crispy rice cereal
- 2 cups candy corn
- ¾ cup mini chocolate chips

Directions

Step 1

Butter a 10x15 baking pan.

Step 2

Melt marshmallows and butter together in a large saucepan over medium heat, stirring until mixture is smooth, about 10 minutes.

Step 3

Combine cereal, candy corn, and chocolate chips together in a large bowl. Add marshmallow mixture to cereal mixture and stir together until cereal is well coated. Spread in prepared pan. Cool to room temperature and cut into squares.

Nutrition Facts

Per Serving:

225.2 calories; protein 1g 2% DV; carbohydrates 42.9g 14% DV; fat 5.6g 9% DV; cholesterol 10.2mg 3% DV; sodium 141.9mg 6% DV.

Halloween Mummy Cookies

Prep: 1 hr **Cook:** 10 mins **Additional:** 45 mins **Total:** 1 hr 55 mins **Servings:** 30 **Yield:** 30 cookies

Ingredients

- ⅔ cup butter, softened
- 1 cup white sugar
- 2 large eggs eggs
- 2 teaspoons vanilla extract
- 2 ½ cups all-purpose flour
- ½ cup unsweetened cocoa powder
- ¼ teaspoon baking soda
- ½ teaspoon salt
- 2 (11 ounce) packages white chocolate chips, or as needed
- 1 ½ tablespoons solid vegetable shortening, or as needed
- miniature chocolate chips

Directions

Step 1

Beat butter and sugar with electric mixer in a large bowl until smooth. Mix in eggs one at a time, beating the first egg in until fully incorporated before adding the second. Stir in vanilla extract.

Step 2

Sift together flour, cocoa powder, baking soda, and salt in a bowl; stir into butter mixture. Shape dough into a log and wrap with waxed paper, parchment, or plastic wrap. Refrigerate until firm, about 30 minutes.

Step 3

Preheat oven to 350 degrees F (175 degrees C).

Step 4

Slice pieces off the log and shape them into narrow wedges about 3 inches long. Set cookies on baking tray. Cut more slices and pull off teaspoon-sized pieces and roll into balls; flatten and press balls onto wide ends of wedges for the mummies' "heads."

Step 5

Bake in preheated until cookies are set and edges are dry, about 8 minutes. Let cool in pan for 1 minute; remove to wire rack to cool completely.

Step 6

Combine white chocolate chips with vegetable shortening in a microwave-safe bowl. Heat in microwave on low until melted, 1 to 2 minutes, stirring every 20 seconds, until coating is warm and smooth. Coat the tops of each cookie with melted white chocolate using a small spatula or butter knife. Reheat white chocolate mixture in microwave for a few seconds and stir again if it becomes too thick to work with. Repeat coating remaining cookies with white chocolate.

Step 7

Use a toothpick to score lines for "bandages" on each cookie, and place mini chocolate chips on the mummy heads for eyes.

Nutrition Facts

Per Serving:

237.2 calories; protein 3.3g 7% DV; carbohydrates 28g 9% DV; fat 13g 20% DV; cholesterol 27.6mg 9% DV; sodium 105.4mg 4% DV.

Huge Scary Spiders

Servings: 10 **Yield:** 20 cookies

Ingredients

- 2 (1 ounce) squares unsweetened chocolate
- 1 ¼ cups all-purpose flour
- 1 ½ teaspoons baking powder
- ¼ teaspoon salt
- ¼ cup butter
- 1 cup white sugar
- 1 egg
- 1 teaspoon vanilla extract
- 40 eaches cinnamon red hot candies

Directions

Step 1

Preheat oven to 375 degrees F (190 degrees C). Lightly grease baking sheet.

Step 2

In a saucepan melt chocolate over low heat. Let cool.

Step 3

In a small bowl mix flour, baking powder and salt.

Step 4

In a medium bowl beat margarine on low speed until smooth. Add sugar and beat until creamy. Stir in egg, vanilla and chocolate. Add flour mixture and mix well, forming a stiff dough.

Step 5

To make spider, shape a 2 inch flat oval for the body. Make the spider's head by flattening a circle about 1/2 inch wide. Shape dough for legs each about 2 inches long and less than 1/4 inch wide.

Step 6

Attach the head and legs to body. Put two red candies into head for eyes. Bake for 5-8 minutes. Let spiders cool on baking sheet to avoid breaking when moving.

Nutrition Facts

Per Serving:

216.5 calories; protein 3g 6% DV; carbohydrates 35.1g 11% DV; fat 8.2g 13% DV; cholesterol 30.8mg 10% DV; sodium 173.1mg 7% DV.

Pumpkin-Pine Cookies

Prep: 10 mins **Cook:** 8 mins **Additional:** 8 mins **Total:** 26 mins **Servings:** 60 **Yield:** 5 dozen

Ingredients

- 2 cups all-purpose flour
- ½ teaspoon baking soda
- ½ teaspoon baking powder
- 1 teaspoon ground cinnamon
- ¼ teaspoon ground cloves
- ½ cup butter, softened
- 1 ⅓ cups white sugar
- 1 egg
- 1 ½ cups canned pumpkin puree
- ¼ cup heavy cream
- 1 cup rolled oats
- ½ cup crushed pineapple, drained
- 1 cup chopped pecans

Directions

Step 1

Preheat the oven to 400 degrees F (200 degrees C). Grease cookie sheets. Stir together the flour, baking soda, baking powder, cinnamon and cloves; set aside.

Step 2

In a large bowl, cream together the butter, sugar and egg until smooth. Stir in the pumpkin and cream. Gradually mix in the dry ingredients until well blended and then stir in the oats, pineapple and pecans. Drop dough by tablespoonfuls onto the prepared cookie sheets.

Step 3

Bake for 8 to 10 minutes in the preheated oven, until bottoms begin to brown. Allow cookies to cool on baking sheets for a few minutes before removing to wire racks to cool completely.

Nutrition Facts

Candy Bar Squares

Servings: 12 **Yield:** 2 dozen

Ingredients

- 1 cup butter, softened
- 1 cup white sugar
- ½ cup packed brown sugar
- 2 large eggs eggs
- 3 cups all-purpose flour
- 1 teaspoon baking soda
- 1 teaspoon salt
- 6 (2.1 ounce) bars chocolate-coated peanut and nougat candy (such as Baby Ruth(R))

Directions

Step 1

Preheat oven to 350 degrees F (175 degrees C).

Step 2

Beat the butter or margarine with the white and brown sugars until light and fluffy. Blend in the eggs, mixing well.

Step 3

Mix in the flour, baking soda and salt to the egg mixture. Reserve 1/2 cup of the chopped candy bars for the topping. Stir the remaining candy into the flour mixture. Spread the batter into one 13x9 inch baking pan. Sprinkle the reserved candy on top.

Step 4

Bake at 350 degrees F (175 degrees C) for 25 to 30 minutes or until lightly browned. Cool in pan on a wire rack then cut into squares.

Nutrition Facts

Per Serving:

504.9 calories; protein 6.7g 13% DV; carbohydrates 69.1g 22% DV; fat 22.8g 35% DV; cholesterol 72.9mg 24% DV; sodium 490.3mg 20% DV.

Oats and Pumpkin Pinwheels

Servings: 24 **Yield:** 4 dozen

Ingredients

- 1 ½ cups all-purpose flour
- 1 cup rolled oats
- ¼ teaspoon baking soda
- 1 ½ cups white sugar
- ½ cup butter, softened
- 2 large egg whites egg whites
- 1 cup canned pumpkin
- ½ teaspoon pumpkin pie spice
- ⅓ cup sesame seeds

Directions

Step 1

In small bowl, combine flour, oats and baking soda; set aside. In large mixing bowl, beat 1 cup sugar and butter or margarine until fluffy; mix in egg whites. Stir in dry ingredients. On waxed paper, press dough into 16 x 12 inch rectangle.

Step 2

In small bowl, combine pumpkin, remaining 1/2 cup sugar and pumpkin pie spice; mix well. Spread mixture over dough to 1/2 inch of edge. Roll dough, beginning at the narrow end. Sprinkle sesame seeds over roll, pressing gently into dough. Wrap in waxed paper; freeze until firm or overnight.

Step 3

Preheat oven to 400 degrees F (200 degrees C).

Step 4

Spray cookie sheet with non-stick cooking spray. Cut frozen dough into 1/4 inch slices; place on cookie sheet. Bake 9 - 11 minutes or until golden brown. Remove to wire rack; cool completely.

Nutrition Facts

Per Serving:

139.9 calories; protein 2.1g 4% DV; carbohydrates 22.1g 7% DV; fat 5.2g 8% DV; cholesterol 10.2mg 3% DV; sodium 70.2mg 3% DV.

Pumpkin Bars IV

Prep: 10 mins **Cook:** 25 mins **Total:** 35 mins **Servings:** 48 **Yield:** 48 bars

Ingredients

- 4 large eggs eggs
- 1 cup vegetable oil
- 2 cups white sugar
- 1 (15 ounce) can pumpkin puree
- 2 cups all-purpose flour
- 2 teaspoons baking powder
- 1 teaspoon baking soda
- ½ teaspoon salt
- 2 teaspoons ground cinnamon
- ½ teaspoon ground ginger
- ½ teaspoon ground cloves
- ½ teaspoon ground nutmeg

Directions

Step 1

Preheat oven to 350 degrees F (175 degrees C). Grease a 12x18 inch half sheet pan.

Step 2

In a large bowl, using a wooden spoon, mix together the eggs, oil, sugar and pumpkin until well blended. Combine the flour, baking powder, baking soda, salt, cinnamon, ginger, cloves and nutmeg; stir into the pumpkin mixture until just blended. Spread evenly into the prepared pan.

Step 3

Bake for 25 to 30 minutes in the preheated oven, until bars spring back when lightly touched. Cool before cutting into bars.

Nutrition Facts

Per Serving:

100.9 calories; protein 1.2g 2% DV; carbohydrates 13.2g 4% DV; fat 5g 8% DV; cholesterol 15.5mg 5% DV; sodium 92.8mg 4% DV.

Jack-O'-Crispies

Prep: 30 mins **Cook:** 5 mins **Additional:** 20 mins **Total:** 55 mins **Servings:** 24 **Yield:** 24 small jack-o-crispies

Ingredients

- 3 tablespoons butter
- 6 cups miniature marshmallows
- 1 teaspoon vanilla extract
- 6 drops orange food coloring, or as needed
- 4 cups crispy rice cereal (such as Rice Krispies), or more to taste

- 6 pieces green licorice string, or as needed
- 1 (.75 ounce) package green fruit roll-up (such as General Mills Fruit Roll-Ups)
- 1 (.75 ounce) tube black decorating gel

Directions

Step 1

Melt butter in a saucepan over low heat. Add marshmallows and vanilla extract. Stir in food coloring. Add rice cereal, 1 cup at a time, stirring after each addition, until blended. Scoop out mixture and shape into small pumpkins using buttered hands.

Step 2

Cut string candy into stems and cut fruit roll-up into leaves. Decorate pumpkins while still soft. Let cool completely, at least 20 minutes. Draw faces onto pumpkins using decorating gel.

Nutrition Facts

Per Serving:

89.3 calories; protein 0.4g 1% DV; carbohydrates 17.8g 6% DV; fat 1.5g 2% DV; cholesterol 3.8mg 1% DV; sodium 79.8mg 3% DV.

Pattern Cookies

Servings: 12 **Yield:** 2 dozen

Ingredients

- ⅔ cup shortening
- 1 cup white sugar
- 2 large eggs eggs
- 1 teaspoon vanilla extract
- ⅓ cup milk
- 3 cups all-purpose flour
- 1 tablespoon baking powder
- ½ teaspoon salt

Directions

Step 1

In a medium bowl, cream together the shortening and sugar. Beat in the eggs, one at a time, then stir in the vanilla and milk. Combine the flour , baking powder and salt, stir into the wet mixture. Cover and chill for about 1 hour.

Step 2

Preheat oven to 350 degrees F (175 degrees C). Line baking sheets with parchment paper. On a lightly floured surface, roll dough out to 1/4 to 1/8 inch thickness. Cut into desired shapes with cookie cutters.

Step 3

Bake for 8 to 10 minutes in the preheated oven, until middle of cookie springs back when touched. Cool on wire racks. Frost with frosting if desired.

Nutrition Facts

Per Serving:

295.7 calories; protein 4.5g 9% DV; carbohydrates 41.3g 13% DV; fat 12.6g 20% DV; cholesterol 31.5mg 11% DV; sodium 233.9mg 9% DV.

Halloween Vegan Yacon Syrup Cookies

Prep: 25 mins **Cook:** 10 mins **Total:** 35 mins **Servings:** 30 **Yield:** 30 cookies

Ingredients

Cookies:

- 2 ½ cups gluten-free flour
- 1 teaspoon baking soda
- ½ teaspoon ground ginger
- ½ teaspoon ground cinnamon
- ¼ teaspoon ground nutmeg
- 1 dash salt
- ½ cup coconut oil, or more as needed
- ½ cup yacon syrup

Icing:

- ¼ cup yacon syrup
- 2 ½ tablespoons melted dark chocolate (85% cacao)

Directions

Step 1

Preheat the oven to 340 degrees F (170 degrees C). Line a baking sheet with parchment paper.

Step 2

Combine flour, baking soda, ginger, cinnamon, nutmeg, and salt in a large bowl. Combine coconut oil and yacon syrup in a separate bowl. Add oil mixture to dry ingredients and mix until dough forms.

Step 3

Roll dough out to about 1/2-inch thickness. Use Halloween-themed cookie cutters to cut out cookies; place them on the prepared baking sheet.

Step 4

Bake in the preheated oven for 10 minutes.

Step 5

While cookies bake, combine yacon syrup and melted chocolate.

Step 6

Remove cookies from oven and apply icing while still hot.

Nutrition Facts

Per Serving:

91.8 calories; protein 1.2g 2% DV; carbohydrates 13.1g 4% DV; fat 4.4g 7% DV; cholesterol 0.1mg; sodium 55mg 2% DV.

Pumpkin Spice Pudding Cookies

Prep: 15 mins **Cook:** 20 mins **Additional:** 5 mins **Total:** 40 mins **Servings:** 36 **Yield:** 3 dozen cookies

Ingredients

- 2 ¼ cups all-purpose flour
- 1 (3.4 ounce) package instant pumpkin-spice pudding mix (such as Jello)
- 1 teaspoon baking soda
- ½ teaspoon pumpkin pie spice
- ½ teaspoon salt
- ¾ cup softened butter
- ½ cup canned pumpkin
- ½ cup white sugar
- ½ cup brown sugar
- 2 eaches eggs
- 1 tablespoon honey
- 1 teaspoon vanilla extract
- 1 cup white chocolate chips
- 1 (14 ounce) package pumpkin-spice flavored candy-coated milk chocolate pieces (such as M&Ms)

Directions

Step 1

Preheat the oven to 350 degrees F (175 degrees C).

Step 2

Combine flour, pudding mix, baking soda, pumpkin pie spice, and salt in a bowl.

Step 3

Combine butter, pumpkin, white sugar, and brown sugar in a large bowl; beat with an electric mixer until fluffy. Beat in eggs, honey, and vanilla extract until incorporated. Mix in the dry ingredients slowly, being careful not to overmix. Stir in the white chocolate chips and pumpkin spice-flavored candies by hand. Drop tablespoonfuls of dough 2 inches apart onto ungreased baking sheets.

Step 4

Bake in the preheated oven until edges are browned and set, about 10 minutes. Cool on the baking sheets for 3 to 4 minutes before removing to a wire rack to cool completely.

Nutrition Facts

Per Serving:

183.9 calories; protein 2.1g 4% DV; carbohydrates 25.7g 8% DV; fat 8.3g 13% DV; cholesterol 21.9mg 7% DV; sodium 149.3mg 6% DV.

Cupcake

Owl Cupcakes

Prep: 30 mins **Cook:** 12 mins **Additional:** 20 mins **Total:** 1 hr 2 mins **Servings:** 24 **Yield:**

24 cupcakes

Ingredients

Cupcakes:

- 2 cups white sugar
- 2 cups all-purpose flour, sifted
- 1 cup unsweetened cocoa powder
- 2 teaspoons baking powder
- 1 teaspoon salt
- ½ teaspoon baking soda

- 1 cup buttermilk
- ½ cup vegetable oil
- 2 large eggs eggs
- 1 teaspoon vanilla extract
- 1 cup hot water

Frosting:

- ¾ cup heavy whipping cream
- 1 ½ tablespoons heavy whipping cream
- 1 ½ cups mascarpone cheese
- 2 tablespoons mascarpone cheese
- 7 tablespoons unsweetened cocoa powder
- ¼ cup white sugar
- Decoration:

- 48 cookies chocolate sandwich cookies (such as Oreo)
- 48 piece (blank)s brown candy-coated milk chocolate pieces (such as M&M's)
- 24 piece (blank)s orange or yellow candy-coated milk chocolate pieces (such as M&M's)

Directions

Step 1

Preheat oven to 350 degrees F (175 degrees C). Line 2 muffin tins with paper liners.

Step 2

Combine 2 cups sugar, flour, 1 cup cocoa powder, baking powder, salt, and baking soda in a bowl.

Step 3

Whisk buttermilk, vegetable oil, eggs, and vanilla extract in a large bowl. Add flour mixture; mix until well-combined. Pour in hot water; stir until batter is smooth. Divide batter evenly among muffin tins.

Step 4

Bake in the preheated oven until a toothpick inserted into the center comes out clean, about 12 minutes. Transfer cupcakes to a wire rack and let cool completely, about 20 minutes.

Step 5

Whip 3/4 cup plus 1 1/2 tablespoon heavy cream in a bowl with an electric mixer until soft peaks form. Fold in 1 1/2 cup plus 2 tablespoons mascarpone cheese, 7 tablespoons cocoa powder, and 1/4 cup sugar gently to make frosting.

Step 6

Spread 1 tablespoon frosting over each cooled cupcake.

Step 7

Twist chocolate sandwich cookies open, leaving all cream filling on 1 side. Place 2 cookies, cream filling-side up, on each cupcake to make owl eyes. Place a brown milk chocolate piece on each cookie to create pupils. Insert an orange or yellow milk chocolate piece in the center to make a beak.

Nutrition Facts

Per Serving:

372.1 calories; protein 5.4g 11% DV; carbohydrates 46.4g 15% DV; fat 20.3g 31% DV; cholesterol 46.7mg 16% DV; sodium 291.3mg 12% DV.

Halloween Fondant Ghost Cupcakes

Prep: 40 mins **Cook:** 16 mins **Additional:** 2 hrs 15 mins **Total:** 3 hrs 11 mins **Servings:**

12 **Yield:** 12 cupcakes

Ingredients

- 1 cup all-purpose flour
- 2 tablespoons all-purpose flour
- ½ cup unsweetened cocoa powder
- 1 teaspoon baking soda
- 1 teaspoon salt
- 1 cup white sugar
- ½ cup butter
- 1 egg
- 1 teaspoon vanilla extract
- 1 cup milk

Decorating:

- 1 (16 ounce) package vanilla frosting
- 6 eaches large marshmallows, cut in half crosswise
- 2 tablespoons confectioners' sugar, or as needed
- 8 ounces ready-to-use white fondant
- 12 eaches raisins, halved

Directions

Step 1

Preheat oven to 350 degrees F (175 degrees C). Grease a 12-cup muffin tin or line cups with paper liners.

Step 2

Sift 1 cup plus 2 tablespoons flour, cocoa powder, baking soda, and salt together in a bowl.

Step 3

Combine sugar and butter in a large bowl; beat with an electric mixer until light and fluffy. Beat in egg and vanilla extract. Mix in flour mixture alternately with milk. Beat until batter is just blended.

Step 4

Bake in the preheated oven until tops spring back when lightly pressed and a toothpick inserted into the center comes out clean, 16 to 20 minutes. Remove from oven and cool on a wire rack for 15 minutes. Remove cupcakes from tin and cool completely, about 2 hours.

Step 5

Frost each cupcake with a thin layer of white vanilla frosting. Place 1 marshmallow half, cut-side up, in the center of each cupcake.

Step 6

Dust a work surface with confectioners' sugar. Pinch off walnut-sized pieces of white fondant; roll into thin circles that are slightly bigger than the cupcakes. Drape over the marshmallows so they look like ghosts. Poke 2 holes near the top for the eyes. Stuff 1 raisin half into each hole.

Nutrition Facts

Per Serving:

454.3 calories; protein 3.2g 6% DV; carbohydrates 75.6g 24% DV; fat 16.4g 25% DV; cholesterol 35.6mg 12% DV; sodium 441.4mg 18% DV.

Chocolate Cupcakes with Pumpkin Cheesecake Filling

Prep: 15 mins **Cook:** 25 mins **Total:** 40 mins **Servings:** 12 **Yield:** 12 cupcakes

Ingredients

Filling:

- 1 (8 ounce) package cream cheese, at room temperature
- ⅓ cup white sugar
- 1 egg
- 2 tablespoons 100% pure pumpkin
- 6 drops yellow food coloring
- 3 drops red food coloring
- ⅛ teaspoon salt
- ½ cup semisweet chocolate chips, or more to taste

Cake:

- 1 ½ cups all-purpose flour
- 1 cup white sugar
- ¼ cup unsweetened cocoa powder
- 1 teaspoon baking soda
- ½ teaspoon salt

- ⅓ cup vegetable oil
- 1 cup water
- 1 teaspoon white vinegar
- 1 teaspoon vanilla extract

Directions

Step 1

Preheat oven to 350 degrees F (175 degrees C). Line a muffin tin with paper liners.

Step 2

Place cream cheese, 1/3 cup sugar, egg, pumpkin, yellow food coloring, red food coloring, and salt in a bowl. Beat using an electric mixer until thoroughly combined and no lumps remain. Stir in chocolate chips.

Step 3

Whisk flour, 1 cup sugar, cocoa powder, baking soda, and 1/2 teaspoon salt together in a large bowl. Mix in water, oil, vinegar, and vanilla extract until batter is well blended.

Step 4

Fill muffin cups 1/2-full with batter; top with 1 tablespoon of the cream cheese mixture. Sprinkle a few chocolate chips on top.

Step 5

Bake in the preheated oven until a toothpick inserted into the center comes out clean, about 25 minutes.

Nutrition Facts

Per Serving:

306.2 calories; protein 4.2g 8% DV; carbohydrates 40.1g 13% DV; fat 15.5g 24% DV; cholesterol 36mg 12% DV; sodium 289.2mg 12% DV.

Pumpkin Ginger Cupcakes

Prep: 20 mins **Cook:** 20 mins **Additional:** 50 mins **Total:** 1 hr 30 mins **Servings:** 24 **Yield:** 24 cupcakes

Ingredients

- 2 cups all-purpose flour
- 1 (3.4 ounce) package instant butterscotch pudding mix

- 2 teaspoons baking soda
- ¼ teaspoon salt
- 1 tablespoon ground cinnamon

- ½ teaspoon ground ginger
- ½ teaspoon ground allspice
- ¼ teaspoon ground cloves
- ⅓ cup finely chopped crystallized ginger
- 1 cup butter, room temperature
- 1 cup white sugar
- 1 cup packed brown sugar
- 4 large eggs eggs, room temperature
- 1 teaspoon vanilla extract
- 1 (15 ounce) can pumpkin puree

Directions

Step 1

Preheat an oven to 350 degrees F (175 degrees C). Grease 24 muffin cups, or line with paper muffin liners. Whisk together the flour, pudding mix, baking soda, salt, cinnamon, ground ginger, allspice, cloves, and crystallized ginger in a bowl; set aside.

Step 2

Beat the butter, white sugar, and brown sugar with an electric mixer in a large bowl until light and fluffy. The mixture should be noticeably lighter in color. Add the eggs one at a time, allowing each egg to blend into the butter mixture before adding the next. Beat in the vanilla and pumpkin puree with the last egg. Stir in the flour mixture, mixing until just incorporated. Pour the batter into the prepared muffin cups.

Step 3

Bake in the preheated oven until golden and the tops spring back when lightly pressed, about 20 minutes. Cool in the pans for 10 minutes before removing to cool completely on a wire rack.

Nutrition Facts

Per Serving:

210.6 calories; protein 2.4g 5% DV; carbohydrates 31.8g 10% DV; fat 8.7g 13% DV; cholesterol 51.3mg 17% DV; sodium 303.2mg 12% DV.

Bat Cupcakes

Prep: 10 mins **Cook:** 20 mins **Total:** 30 mins **Servings:** 24 **Yield:** 2 dozen

Ingredients

- 1 (18.25 ounce) package chocolate cake mix
- 1 (16 ounce) container prepared chocolate frosting
- 1 (11.5 ounce) package fudge stripe cookies
- 1 (6 ounce) bag milk chocolate candy kisses, unwrapped
- 1 tablespoon red gel icing

Directions

Step 1

Prepare the cake mix according to package directions for cupcakes. Cool. Frost cupcakes with chocolate frosting.

Step 2

Break the cookies in half, and press two halves into the top of each cupcake for wings, stripes facing the frosting. Place a chocolate kiss in front of the cookies with the point facing forward for the body. Make two beady little eyes with the red gel icing towards the point of the kiss. Let the fun begin!

Nutrition Facts

Per Serving:

272.6 calories; protein 2.8g 6% DV; carbohydrates 41g 13% DV; fat 11.8g 18% DV; cholesterol 1.5mg 1% DV; sodium 271.9mg 11% DV.

Cupcake Graveyard

Prep: 30 mins **Cook:** 25 mins **Total:** 55 mins **Servings:** 24 **Yield:** 2 dozen

Ingredients

- 1 (18.25 ounce) package chocolate cake mix
- 2 (16 ounce) packages vanilla frosting
- ¾ cup chocolate sandwich cookie crumbs
- 24 eaches chocolate covered graham cracker cookies

Directions

Step 1

Prepare and bake cake mix according to package directions for cupcakes.

Step 2

In a medium bowl stir 1 package of frosting with the cookie crumbs. Frost cooled cupcakes.

Step 3

Fill a pastry bag, fitted with a plain tip, with remaining white frosting. Write R.I.P. on each chocolate covered graham cracker cookie. Stand a decorated cookie on top of each cupcake so that it looks like a tombstone. Place the cupcakes on a large cookie sheet that has been covered with green paper. Place paper ghosts and bats randomly through the graveyard. Serve!

Nutrition Facts

Per Serving:

311.5 calories; protein 1.7g 4% DV; carbohydrates 49.3g 16% DV; fat 12.4g 19% DV; cholesterolmg; sodium 284mg 11% DV.

Creepy Halloween Skull Cupcakes

Prep: 30 mins **Cook:** 18 mins **Additional:** 1 hr 45 mins **Total:** 2 hrs 33 mins **Servings:** 24 **Yield:** 24 cupcakes

Ingredients

- 1 (18.25 ounce) package devil's food cake mix (such as Duncan Hines)
- 1 cup water
- 3 eaches eggs
- ⅓ cup vegetable oil
- 1 ½ (16 ounce) packages prepared vanilla frosting
- 1 (7 ounce) pouch prepared chocolate frosting

Directions

Step 1

Preheat oven to 350 degrees F (175 degrees C). Line two 12-cup muffin tins with paper liners, preferable dark-colored or Halloween-themed ones.

Step 2

Combine cake mix, water, eggs, and oil in a large bowl; beat with an electric mixer on low speed until moistened, about 30 seconds. Beat at medium speed until batter is smooth and creamy, about 2 minutes. Spoon batter into the prepared muffin cups, filling each 3/4 full.

Step 3

Bake in the preheated oven until a toothpick inserted in the center comes out clean, 18 to 21 minutes. Remove from oven and cool tins on a wire rack for 15 minutes. Remove cupcakes from the tins and cool completely on a wire rack before decorating, about 1 hour.

Step 4

Frost each cupcake with a thin layer of white vanilla frosting and refrigerate for 30 minutes to make decorating easier.

Step 5

Remove cupcakes from fridge and apply a second layer of white frosting. Fill a piping bag outfitted with a small round tip with chocolate frosting and draw a skull face on the cupcakes: pipe large ovals for the eyes, two dots for the nostrils, and a large "stitched" smile for the mouth.

Nutrition Facts

Per Serving:

275.8 calories; protein 2.8g 6% DV; carbohydrates 38.6g 13% DV; fat 13.1g 20% DV; cholesterol 24.7mg 8% DV; sodium 234.4mg 9% DV.

Pumpkin Spice Cupcakes With Cream Cheese Frosting

Prep: 20 mins **Cook:** 20 mins **Additional:** 10 mins **Total:** 50 mins **Servings:** 24 **Yield:** 2 dozen cupcakes

Ingredients

Cupcakes:

- 2 ½ cups white sugar
- ¾ cup butter, softened
- 3 large eggs eggs
- 1 (15 ounce) can solid-pack pumpkin puree
- 2 ⅓ cups all-purpose flour
- 1 tablespoon pumpkin pie spice
- 1 tablespoon ground cinnamon
- ¾ teaspoon baking powder
- ½ teaspoon ground ginger
- 1 cup buttermilk

Frosting:

- 1 (8 ounce) package cream cheese, softened
- ½ cup butter, softened
- 4 cups confectioners' sugar
- 2 teaspoons ground cinnamon
- 1 teaspoon vanilla extract

Directions

Step 1

Preheat oven to 350 degrees F (175 degrees C). Line 24 muffin cups with paper liners.

Step 2

Beat white sugar and 3/4 cup butter together in a bowl using an electric mixer until smooth and creamy; add eggs, 1 at a time, beating well after each addition. Beat pumpkin into creamed butter mixture.

Step 3

Mix flour, pumpkin pie spice, 1 tablespoon cinnamon, baking powder, and ginger together in a bowl; stir into creamed butter mixture, alternating with buttermilk, until batter is smooth. Fill each muffin cup 3/4-full with batter.

Step 4

Bake in the preheated oven until a toothpick inserted in the center of a cupcake comes out clean, 20 to 25 minutes. Cool in muffin tin for 10 minutes before transferring to wire rack.

Step 5

Beat cream cheese and 1/2 cup butter together in a bowl using an electric mixer until fluffy. Beat confectioners' sugar, 2 teaspoons cinnamon, and vanilla extract into creamed butter until frosting is smooth. Spread frosting on each cupcake.

Nutrition Facts

Per Serving:

345.3 calories; protein 3.4g 7% DV; carbohydrates 53.8g 17% DV; fat 13.8g 21% DV; cholesterol 59.3mg 20% DV; sodium 173.9mg 7% DV.

Pumpkin Spice Cupcakes

Prep: 25 mins **Cook:** 25 mins **Additional:** 50 mins **Total:** 1 hr 40 mins **Servings:** 24 **Yield:** 24 cupcakes

Ingredients

- 2 ¼ cups all-purpose flour
- 1 teaspoon ground cinnamon
- ½ teaspoon ground nutmeg
- ½ teaspoon ground ginger
- ½ teaspoon ground cloves
- ½ teaspoon ground allspice
- ½ teaspoon salt
- 1 tablespoon baking powder
- ½ teaspoon baking soda
- ½ cup butter, softened
- 1 cup white sugar
- ⅓ cup brown sugar
- 2 large eggs eggs, room temperature
- ¾ cup milk
- 1 cup pumpkin puree
- Cinnamon Cream Cheese Frosting
- 1 (8 ounce) package cream cheese, softened
- ¼ cup butter, softened
- 3 cups confectioners' sugar
- 1 teaspoon vanilla extract
- 1 teaspoon ground cinnamon

Directions

Step 1

Preheat an oven to 375 degrees F (190 degrees C). Grease 24 muffin cups, or line with paper muffin liners. Sift together the flour, 1 teaspoon cinnamon, nutmeg, ginger, clove, allspice, salt, baking powder, and baking soda; set aside.

Step 2

Beat 1/2 cup of butter, the white sugar, and brown sugar with an electric mixer in a large bowl until light and fluffy. The mixture should be noticeably lighter in color. Add the room-temperature eggs one at a time, allowing each egg to blend into the butter mixture before adding the next. Stir in the milk and pumpkin puree after the last egg. Stir in the flour mixture, mixing until just incorporated. Pour the batter into the prepared muffin cups.

Step 3

Bake in the preheated oven until golden and the tops spring back when lightly pressed, about 25 minutes. Cool in the pans for 5 minutes before removing to cool completely on a wire rack.

Step 4

While the cupcakes are cooling, make the frosting by beating the cream cheese and 1/4 butter with an electric mixer in a bowl until smooth. Beat in the confectioners' sugar a little at a time until incorporated. Add the vanilla extract and 1 teaspoon ground cinnamon; beat until fluffy. Once the cupcakes are cool, frost with the cream cheese icing.

Nutrition Facts

Per Serving:

243.9 calories; protein 2.9g 6% DV; carbohydrates 37.2g 12% DV; fat 9.8g 15% DV; cholesterol 41.6mg 14% DV; sodium 220.1mg 9% DV.

Carrot Cupcakes with White Chocolate Cream Cheese Icing

Prep: 30 mins **Cook:** 25 mins **Additional:** 1 hr **Total:** 1 hr 55 mins **Servings:** 12 **Yield:** 12 muffins

Ingredients

Cream Cheese Icing:

- 2 ounces white chocolate
- 1 (8 ounce) package cream cheese, softened
- ½ cup unsalted butter, softened
- 1 teaspoon vanilla extract
- ½ teaspoon orange extract
- 4 cups confectioners' sugar
- 2 tablespoons heavy cream

Carrot Cake:

- 2 large eggs eggs, lightly beaten
- 1 ⅛ cups white sugar
- ⅓ cup brown sugar
- ½ cup vegetable oil
- 1 teaspoon vanilla extract
- 2 cups shredded carrots
- ½ cup crushed pineapple
- 1 ½ cups all-purpose flour
- 1 ¼ teaspoons baking soda
- ½ teaspoon salt
- 1 ½ teaspoons ground cinnamon
- ½ teaspoon ground nutmeg
- ¼ teaspoon ground ginger
- 1 cup chopped walnuts

Directions

Step 1

Preheat oven to 350 degrees F (175 degrees C). Lightly grease 12 muffin cups.

Step 2

In small saucepan, melt white chocolate over low heat. Stir until smooth, and allow to cool to room temperature.

Step 3

In a bowl, beat together the cream cheese and butter until smooth. Mix in white chocolate, 1 teaspoon vanilla, and orange extract. Gradually beat in the confectioners' sugar until the mixture is fluffy. Mix in heavy cream.

Step 4

Beat together the eggs, white sugar, and brown sugar in a bowl, and mix in the oil and vanilla. Fold in carrots and pineapple. In a separate bowl, mix the flour, baking soda, salt, cinnamon, nutmeg, and ginger. Mix flour mixture into the carrot mixture until evenly moist. Fold in 1/2 cup walnuts. Transfer to the prepared muffin cups.

Step 5

Bake 25 minutes in the preheated oven, or until a toothpick inserted in the center of a muffin comes out clean. Cool completely on wire racks before topping with the icing and sprinkling with remaining walnuts.

Nutrition Facts

Per Serving:

639.1 calories; protein 6g 12% DV; carbohydrates 84.7g 27% DV; fat 32.2g 50% DV; cholesterol 76.2mg 25% DV; sodium 317.4mg 13% DV.

Harvest Pumpkin Cupcakes

Prep: 20 mins **Cook:** 30 mins **Additional:** 30 mins **Total:** 1 hr 20 mins **Servings:** 32 **Yield:**

32 servings

Ingredients

Cupcakes:

- 4 large eggs eggs, slightly beaten
- ¾ cup Mazola Vegetable Plus! Oil
- 2 cups sugar
- 1 (15 ounce) can pumpkin
- 1 ¾ cups all-purpose flour
- ¼ cup Argo OR Kingsford's Corn Starch
- 4 teaspoons Spice Islands Pumpkin Pie Spice
- 2 teaspoons Argo Baking Powder
- 1 teaspoon baking soda
- ¾ teaspoon salt

Frosting:

- 1 (8 ounce) package cream cheese, softened
- 3 tablespoons butter OR margarine, softened
- 1 tablespoon orange juice

- 2 teaspoons Spice Islands 100% Pure Bourbon Vanilla Extract
- 1 ½ teaspoons freshly grated orange peel
- 4 cups powdered sugar

Directions

Step 1

To make cupcakes: Blend the eggs, oil, sugar, and pumpkin in a large mixing bowl; set aside. Stir together dry ingredients in a separate bowl. Add dry ingredients to pumpkin mixture and beat until well blended. POUR into lined muffin tins. Fill about 2/3 full. Bake in preheated 350 degrees oven for 30 minutes or until center springs back when touched. Cool 30 minutes. Spread with frosting.

Step 2

To make frosting: Beat cream cheese and butter until fluffy. Add remaining ingredients and beat until smooth. Spread over cooled cupcakes.

Nutrition Facts

Per Serving:

233.4 calories; protein 2.2g 4% DV; carbohydrates 35.9g 12% DV; fat 9.6g 15% DV; cholesterol 33.8mg 11% DV; sodium 193.9mg 8% DV.

Bloody Broken Glass Cupcakes

Prep: 30 mins **Cook:** 30 mins **Additional:** 20 mins **Total:** 1 hr 20 mins **Servings:** 24 **Yield:**

24 cupcakes

Ingredients

- 1 (18.25 ounce) package white cake mix
- 1 cup water
- ⅓ cup vegetable oil

- 3 large eggs eggs
- 1 (16 ounce) can white frosting

Sugar Glass:

- 2 cups water
- 1 cup light corn syrup
- 3 ½ cups white sugar
- ¼ teaspoon cream of tartar
- Edible Blood:

- ½ cup light corn syrup
- 1 tablespoon cornstarch
- ¼ cup water, or more as needed
- 15 drops red food coloring
- 3 drops blue food coloring

Directions

Step 1

Preheat an oven to 350 degrees F (175 degrees C). Line 2, 12-cupcake tins with paper cupcake liners.

Step 2

Blend cake mix, 1 cup water, vegetable oil, and eggs in a large bowl. Beat with a mixer on low speed for 2 minutes. Divide cake batter between lined cupcake tins.

Step 3

Bake cupcakes in preheated oven until a toothpick inserted in the center comes out clean, 18 to 22 minutes. Cool completely. Frost cupcakes with white frosting.

Step 4

Make the sugar glass. Mix 2 cups water, 1 cup corn syrup, white sugar, and cream of tartar in a large saucepan; bring to a boil. Use a candy thermometer and boil sugar syrup until temperature reaches 300 degrees (hard ball), stirring constantly. The mixture will thicken as water evaporates. When sugar reaches 300 degrees, quickly pour onto a metal baking pan. Cool until completely hardened. Break into "shards" using a meat mallet.

Step 5

Make the edible blood. Mix together 1/2 cup corn syrup and cornstarch in a large bowl. Slowly stir in the 1/4 cup of water, adding more if necessary, until the corn syrup mixture has thickened to the consistency of blood. Stir in the red and blue food coloring.

Step 6

Stab each frosted cupcake with a few shards of broken sugar glass. Drizzle on drops of "blood" to complete the effect.

Nutrition Facts

Per Serving:

376.7 calories; protein 1.7g 4% DV; carbohydrates 74.6g 24% DV; fat 9g 14% DV; cholesterol 23.3mg 8% DV; sodium 198.2mg 8% DV.

Spider Cupcakes

Prep: 1 hr **Cook:** 30 mins **Total:** 1 hr 30 mins **Servings:** 24 **Yield:** 24 cupcakes

Ingredients

- 1 (18.25 ounce) package chocolate cake mix
- 1 pound black shoestring licorice
- 1 (16 ounce) can white frosting
- 48 eaches pieces candy corn

- 48 eaches cinnamon red hot candies
- ¼ cup orange decorator sugar

Directions

Step 1

Prepare cupcakes according to package directions. Let cool completely.

Step 2

Cut licorice into 3 inch sections. Working with one or two cupcakes at a time, so the frosting doesn't set before decorating, frost the cupcakes with the white frosting. Insert licorice pieces into the outer edges of the cupcakes to make the legs of the spider, 3 legs on each side (4 takes up too much space). Place two pieces of candy corn on the front of the cupcake for fangs and use two red hots as eyes. Sprinkle with decorator sugar. Repeat with remaining cupcakes.

Nutrition Facts

Per Serving:

259.5 calories; protein 1.7g 4% DV; carbohydrates 49.8g 16% DV; fat 6.4g 10% DV; cholesterolmg; sodium 241.1mg 10% DV.

Candy Corn Cupcakes

Prep: 15 mins **Cook:** 20 mins **Additional:** 20 mins **Total:** 55 mins **Servings:** 24 **Yield:** 2 dozen cupcakes

Ingredients

- 1 (18.25 ounce) package white cake mix
- 1 cup water
- ⅓ cup vegetable oil
- 3 large eggs eggs
- 14 drops red food coloring, or as needed - divided
- 22 drops yellow food coloring, or as needed - divided
- 6 drops green food coloring, or as needed
- 2 cups prepared white frosting
- 12 eaches pieces of yellow, orange, and white candy corn
- 12 eaches pieces of brown, orange, and white candy corn

Directions

Step 1

Preheat oven to 350 degrees F (175 degrees C). Line 24 cupcake cups with paper liners.

Step 2

Place cake mix in a bowl, and pour in water and vegetable oil; add 3 eggs. With electric mixer on low speed, beat the cake mix with water, oil, and eggs until thoroughly combined, about 2 minutes. Pour half the cake mix into a second bowl; divide the remaining cake mix in half, and place into 2 separate small bowls.

Step 3

Color the largest portion of the cake mix orange by mixing in 4 drops of red food coloring and 6 drops of yellow food coloring. Into a second, smaller bowl of cake mix, mix in 10 drops of red food coloring, 12 drops of yellow food coloring, and 6 drops of green food coloring, to color that bowl brown. Into the last remaining small bowl of cake mix, stir in 5 drops of yellow food coloring to color that bowl yellow.

Step 4

Spoon yellow cake batter into the bottoms of 12 prepared cupcake cups, filling them about 1/3 full. Spoon the brown batter into the bottoms of the remaining 12 prepared cupcake cups, filling them about 1/3 full. Spoon orange cupcake mix over the yellow and brown layers, filling the cupcakes about 2/3 full. Try not to jar or shake the filled cupcakes, to avoid mixing layers.

Step 5

Carefully place cupcakes into the preheated oven, and bake until a toothpick inserted into the center of a cupcake comes out clean, 18 to 22 minutes. Allow to cool.

Step 6

Frost each cooled cupcake with the white frosting; place a piece of yellow, orange, and white candy corn on top of each yellow and orange cupcake. Place a brown, orange, and white piece of candy corn on top of each brown and orange cupcake.

Nutrition Facts

Per Serving:

238.3 calories; protein 2g 4% DV; carbohydrates 35g 11% DV; fat 10.6g 16% DV; cholesterol 23.3mg 8% DV; sodium 199.3mg 8% DV.

Rick's Special Buttercream Frosting

Prep: 30 mins **Total:** 30 mins **Servings:** 12 **Yield:** 7 cups

Ingredients

- 2 cups shortening
- 8 cups confectioners' sugar
- ½ teaspoon salt
- 2 teaspoons vanilla extract
- 1 cup heavy whipping cream

Directions

Step 1

In a mixing bowl, cream shortening until fluffy. Add sugar, and continue creaming until well blended.

Step 2

Add salt, vanilla, and 6 ounces whipping cream. Blend on low speed until moistened. Add additional 2 ounces whipping cream if necessary. Beat at high speed until frosting is fluffy.

Nutrition Facts

Per Serving:

683.7 calories; protein 0.4g 1% DV; carbohydrates 80.3g 26% DV; fat 41.6g 64% DV; cholesterol 27.2mg 9% DV; sodium 105.3mg 4% DV.

Ann's Chocolate Chip Carrot Cake Pumpkins

Prep: 20 mins **Cook:** 20 mins **Additional:** 30 mins **Total:** 1 hr 10 mins **Servings:** 12 **Yield:** 12 servings

Ingredients

Cupcakes:

- 2 cups cake flour
- 2 teaspoons ground cinnamon
- 1 ½ teaspoons baking soda
- 1 teaspoon baking powder
- 1 teaspoon salt
- 2 cups white sugar
- 1 ½ cups vegetable oil
- 4 large eggs eggs
- 2 cups grated carrots
- 1 (8 ounce) can crushed pineapple, drained
- 1 tablespoon cake flour
- ½ cup chopped walnuts
- ½ cup semisweet chocolate chips

Frosting:

- ½ cup butter
- 1 (8 ounce) package cream cheese, softened
- 1 tablespoon vanilla extract
- 2 cups confectioners' sugar, or more as needed
- 1 tablespoon lemon juice
- 3 drops orange food coloring
- 1 (1.5 ounce) tube black decorating gel

Directions

Step 1

Preheat oven to 325 degrees F (165 degrees C). (If using a countertop induction oven, preheat to 325 degrees F.) Grease 12 pumpkin-shaped cupcake molds (silicon molds work well).

Step 2

Sift 2 cups cake flour, cinnamon, baking soda, baking powder, and salt together in a bowl. Mix in sugar, oil, and eggs until combined. Stir carrots and pineapple into the batter.

Step 3

Place 1 tablespoon cake flour in a bowl. Toss walnuts and chocolate chips in flour until coated; fold into batter.

Step 4

Pour batter into cupcake molds to about two-thirds full; gently tap molds onto work surface to remove air bubbles.

Step 5

Bake in preheated oven (or countertop induction oven) until a toothpick inserted into the center of a cupcake comes out clean, 20 to 25 minutes (or 15 to 20 minutes in the countertop induction oven). Cool to room temperature, 15 to 20 minutes; remove from molds.

Step 6

Combine butter, cream cheese, and vanilla extract in a bowl; beat with an electric mixer until well blended, 4 to 6 minutes. Mix in confectioners' sugar on low speed, 1/2 cup at a time, until frosting is smooth and spreadable. Add lemon juice and orange food coloring; stir until combined. Refrigerate until set, 15 to 20 minutes.

Step 7

Frost cupcakes with the cream cheese frosting; decorate with black decorating gel.

Nutrition Facts

Per Serving:

818.3 calories; protein 7.3g 15% DV; carbohydrates 89.4g 29% DV; fat 49.4g 76% DV; cholesterol 102.9mg 34% DV; sodium 595.3mg 24% DV.

Halloween Cyclops Cupcakes

Prep: 30 mins **Cook:** 10 mins **Additional:** 1 hr 30 mins **Total:** 2 hrs 10 mins **Servings:** 12

Yield: 12 cupcakes

Ingredients

Cupcakes:

- 9 tablespoons unsweetened cocoa powder
- 5 tablespoons boiling water, or more if needed

- ¾ cup unsalted butter
- ¾ cup white sugar
- 2 tablespoons white sugar
- 3 eaches eggs
- 1 cup all-purpose flour
- 2 teaspoons baking powder

Frosting:

- 1 (8 ounce) package cream cheese, softened and cubed
- ¼ cup unsalted butter, softened
- ½ teaspoon vanilla extract
- 1 cup confectioners' sugar
- 3 drops green food coloring

Cyclops:

- 1 (.68 oz. tube) black decorating gel
- 12 piece (blank)s blue candy-coated milk chocolate pieces
- 4 eaches marshmallows
- 3 eaches dark colored fruit leather
- 2 tablespoons confectioners' sugar
- ½ teaspoon lemon juice, or more as needed
- 3 tablespoons silver dragees decorating candy
- 24 eaches sunflower seeds

Directions

Step 1

Preheat the oven to 400 degrees F (200 degrees C). Grease a 12-cup muffin tin or line cups with paper liners.

Step 2

Sift cocoa powder into a large bowl and add 5 tablespoons boiling water. Stir into a thick paste, adding more water, 1 tablespoon at a time, if needed. Add 3/4 cup butter and 3/4 cup plus 2 tablespoons sugar and beat with an electric mixer until smooth and creamy. Beat in eggs one at a time, beating well after each addition, until batter is smooth.

Step 3

Mix flour and baking powder in a bowl and stir into the batter until well combined. Spoon batter into the prepared muffin cups, filling each 2/3 to the top using an ice cream scoop.

Step 4

Bake in the preheated oven until tops spring back when lightly pressed and a toothpick comes out clean, 10 to 15 minutes. Allow to cool in muffin tin for a few minutes; transfer to wire rack and cool completely, about 1 hour.

Step 5

Beat cream cheese and 1/4 cup butter together in a bowl until creamy. Mix in vanilla extract. Stir in 1 cup confectioners' sugar gradually until frosting is smooth. Mix in green food coloring.

Step 6

Frost each cupcake with a thin layer of green frosting and refrigerate for 30 minutes to make decorating easier. Frost with a second thin layer of green frosting.

Step 7

Draw a small dot with the black decorating gel on each candy-coated milk chocolate piece for the pupil. Cut marshmallows into 4 slices with a sharp knife and stick 1 blue pupil in the center of each marshmallow piece.

Step 8

Cut fruit leather into crescent shapes or semi-circles for the mouths using small sharp scissors.

Step 9

Mix 2 tablespoons confectioners' sugar with lemon juice in a bowl to make icing. Glue silver dragees onto the fruit leather mouths using a toothpick dipped in icing.

Step 10

Assemble cyclops by placing a mouth and one marshmallow eye onto each cupcake. Stick 2 sunflower seeds on top of the cupcake for the horns.

Nutrition Facts

Per Serving:

424.6 calories; protein 5.3g 11% DV; carbohydrates 48.2g 16% DV; fat 25.2g 39% DV; cholesterol 102.2mg 34% DV; sodium 275.9mg 11% DV.

Halloween Chocolate Cupcakes with Monster Peanut Butter Eyes

Prep: 50 mins **Cook:** 15 mins **Additional:** 2 hrs **Total:** 3 hrs 5 mins **Servings:** 12 **Yield:**

12 cupcakes

Ingredients

Chocolate Cupcakes:

- 9 tablespoons unsweetened cocoa powder
- 5 tablespoons boiling water, or more if needed
- ¾ cup unsalted butter
- ¾ cup white sugar
- 2 tablespoons white sugar
- 1 cup all-purpose flour
- 2 teaspoons baking powder
- 3 eaches eggs
- 1 teaspoon vanilla extract

Peanut Butter Eyes:

- 4 cups confectioners' sugar
- 1 ¾ cups peanut butter
- 1 cup white chocolate chips
- ¼ cup butter
- 1 (1.5 ounce) tube red decorating gel
- 1 (16 ounce) package prepared chocolate frosting
- 1 (1.5 ounce) tube white decorating gel

Directions

Step 1

Preheat oven to 200 degrees F (95 degrees C). Grease a 12-cup muffin tin or line cups with paper liners.

Step 2

Sift cocoa powder into a large bowl and add 5 tablespoons boiling water. Stir into a thick paste, adding more water, 1 tablespoon at a time, if needed. Add 3/4 cup butter and 3/4 cup plus 2 tablespoons sugar and beat with an electric mixer until smooth and creamy. Beat in eggs one at a time, beating well after each addition, until batter is smooth.

Step 3

Mix flour and baking powder in a bowl and stir into the batter until well combined. Spoon batter into the prepared muffin cups, filling each 2/3 to the top using an ice cream scoop.

Step 4

Bake in the preheated oven until tops spring back when lightly pressed and a toothpick comes out clean, 10 to 15 minutes. Allow to cool in muffin tin for a few minutes; transfer to wire rack and cool completely, about 1 hour.

Step 5

Beat confectioners' sugar, peanut butter, 1/4 cup butter, and vanilla extract in a bowl until a thick dough forms. Refrigerate for 30 minutes.

Step 6

Line a baking sheet with baking parchment.

Step 7

Remove the peanut butter mixture from the fridge and roll into small balls to make monster eyes. Chill mixture or moisten hands if it starts to stick. Arrange balls on the prepared baking sheet and freeze for 30 minutes.

Step 8

Place white chocolate in top of a double boiler over simmering water. Stir continuously, scraping down the sides with a rubber spatula to avoid scorching, until chocolate is melted, about 5 minutes.

Step 9

Remove the eyes from the freezer and individually pick them up with a toothpick. Dip balls into melted chocolate leaving a small circle on one side blank. Twirl the toothpick to remove excess chocolate and put back on the parchment lined baking sheet.

Step 10

Dig out a bit of the peanut butter mixture from each ball where it isn't covered with chocolate to make room for the red decorating gel. Fill the holes with red decorating gel.

Step 11

Frost cupcakes with chocolate frosting. Place 2 peanut butter eyes on top. Draw on a mouth with the white decorating gel.

Nutrition Facts

Per Serving:

889.7 calories; protein 14.3g 29% DV; carbohydrates 109.8g 35% DV; fat 48.2g 74% DV; cholesterol 84.8mg 28% DV; sodium 499.6mg 20% DV.

Monster Mini Cupcakes

Prep: 45 mins **Cook:** 14 mins **Additional:** 1 hr 5 mins **Total:** 2 hrs 4 mins **Servings:** 24

Yield: 24 mini cupcakes

Ingredients

Mini Chocolate Cupcakes:

- ½ cup milk
- 1 tablespoon white vinegar
- ½ cup unsalted butter, at room temperature
- 10 tablespoons white sugar
- 2 teaspoons vanilla sugar
- 2 large eggs
- ¾ cup all-purpose flour
- 1 tablespoon all-purpose flour
- ½ cup unsweetened cocoa powder
- ½ teaspoon baking powder
- ¼ teaspoon baking soda
- 1 pinch salt

Cream Cheese Frosting:

- 1 (8 ounce) package cream cheese, softened
- ¼ cup unsalted butter, at room temperature
- 1 teaspoon vanilla extract
- 1 cup confectioners' sugar, sifted
- 2 drops orange food coloring
- 48 eaches small candy eyeballs

- 2 pieces dried mango

Directions

Step 1

Combine milk and vinegar in a bowl. Let stand until milk curdles, about 5 minutes.

Step 2

Preheat oven to 350 degrees F (175 degrees C). Grease a 24-cup mini muffin tin or line cups with paper liners.

Step 3

Combine 1/2 cup butter, white sugar, and vanilla sugar in a large bowl; beat with an electric mixer until smooth and creamy. Add eggs one at a time, beating well after each addition.

Step 4

Mix 3/4 cup plus 1 tablespoon flour, cocoa powder, baking powder, baking soda, and salt in a bowl. Alternate adding flour mixture and curdled milk to the creamed butter mixture, mixing until batter is well blended. Spoon batter into the prepared muffin cups, filling each 3/4 full.

Step 5

Bake in the preheated oven until tops spring back when lightly pressed and a toothpick inserted in the center of 1 cupcake comes back clean, about 14 minutes. Cool in the muffin tin for a few minutes, then transfer to a wire rack to cool completely, about 1 hour.

Step 6

Combine cream cheese and 1/4 cup butter in a bowl; beat with an electric mixer until well combined. Mix in vanilla extract. Stir in confectioners' sugar gradually. Color frosting orange with a few drops of food coloring.

Step 7

Place orange frosting in a pastry bag fitted with a grass tip. Hold the pastry bag at a 90-degree angle 1/8 inch above the surface of a cupcake. Squeeze bag to form orange 'fur' by pulling tip up and away when the icing strand is about 1/2 inch high. Repeat to cover cupcake evenly with fur.

Step 8

Add 2 eyes to each cupcake. Cut dried mango into small strips and arrange into the frosting as 'horns'.

Nutrition Facts

Per Serving:

163.4 calories; protein 2.3g 5% DV; carbohydrates 17g 6% DV; fat 10.2g 16% DV; cholesterol 41.4mg 14% DV; sodium 67.1mg 3% DV.

Vegan Halloween Chocolate Cupcakes with Vegan Matcha Icing

Prep: 30 mins **Cook:** 20 mins **Additional:** 1 hr **Total:** 1 hr 50 mins **Servings:** 12 **Yield:**

12 cupcakes

Ingredients

- 2 ⅓ cups all-purpose flour
- 2 cups white sugar
- ¾ cup dark cocoa powder
- 2 teaspoons baking powder
- 1 teaspoon instant espresso powder
- ½ teaspoon baking soda
- ¼ teaspoon salt
- 1 cup almond milk
- ½ cup canola oil
- 2 teaspoons apple cider vinegar
- 2 teaspoons vanilla extract
- Matcha Vegan Icing:
- 1 cup confectioners' sugar
- 1 teaspoon green tea powder (matcha)
- ½ teaspoon almond extract
- ½ teaspoon vanilla extract
- 1 tablespoon almond milk, or as needed

Directions

Step 1

Preheat the oven to 350 degrees F (175 degrees C). Place liners into a 12-cup muffin tin.

Step 2

Combine flour, sugar, cocoa powder, baking powder, espresso powder, baking soda, and salt in a large bowl. Sift flour mixture into another bowl and sift again back to the first bowl. Add almond milk, oil, vinegar, and vanilla extract and beat using an electric mixer on medium speed until well combined. Fill each lined muffin cup 1/3 full of batter.

Step 3

Bake in the preheated oven until a toothpick inserted in the center of a cupcake comes out clean, 20 to 25 minutes.

Step 4

While cupcakes are baking, sift confectioners' sugar into a bowl and add matcha powder. Whisk together to blend. Add almond extract and vanilla extract and stir to combine. Mix in almond milk 1 teaspoon at a time using a whisk or spoon until icing reaches a good spreading consistency.

Step 5

Allow cupcakes to cool completely before icing, about 1 hour.

Cook's Note:

I use unbleached flour and raw sugar.

Nutrition Facts

Per Serving:

362.7 calories; protein 3.7g 7% DV; carbohydrates 66.4g 21% DV; fat 10.6g 16% DV; cholesterolmg; sodium 198.2mg 8% DV.

Easy Halloween Mummy Cupcakes

Prep: 30 mins **Cook:** 18 mins **Additional:** 1 hr 15 mins **Total:** 2 hrs 3 mins **Servings:** 24 **Yield:** 24 cupcakes

Ingredients

- 1 (18.25 ounce) package devil's food cake mix (such as Duncan Hines)
- 1 cup water
- 3 large eggs eggs
- ⅓ cup vegetable oil
- 1 (16 ounce) can vanilla frosting
- 48 eaches chocolate chips

Directions

Step 1

Preheat oven to 350 degrees F (175 degrees C). Line two 12-cup muffin tins with paper liners, preferable dark-colored or Halloween-themed ones.

Step 2

Combine cake mix, water, eggs, and oil in a large bowl; beat with an electric mixer on low speed until moistened, about 30 seconds. Beat at medium speed until batter is smooth and creamy, about 2 minutes. Spoon batter into the prepared muffin cups, filling each 3/4 full.

Step 3

Bake in the preheated oven until a toothpick inserted in the center comes out clean, 18 to 21 minutes. Remove from oven and cool tins on a wire rack for 15 minutes. Remove cupcakes from the tins and cool completely on a wire rack before decorating, about 1 hour.

Step 4

Spoon frosting in an pastry bag or a plastic bag with the corner cut off. Pipe strands of frosting onto the top and bottom of the cupcakes, leaving an oval eye shape exposed in the middle. Pipe 2 dots in the exposed middle for the mummy's eyes. Place 2 chocolate chips flat-side up in the middle of each dot for the pupils.

Nutrition Facts

Per Serving:

360.7 calories; protein 3.8g 8% DV; carbohydrates 48g 16% DV; fat 19.3g 30% DV; cholesterol 27.5mg 9% DV; sodium 205.2mg 8% DV.

Frankenstein Cupcakes

Prep: 30 mins **Cook:** 20 mins **Additional:** 30 mins **Total:** 1 hr 20 mins **Servings:** 24 **Yield:** 24 cupcakes

Ingredients

Cupcakes:

- 1 (15.25 ounce) package yellow cake mix
- 1 cup water
- 3 large eggs eggs
- ⅓ cup vegetable oil

Frosting:

- 1 cup shortening
- 1 cup butter, softened
- 2 teaspoons vanilla extract
- 8 cups confectioners' sugar
- ⅓ cup milk
- 3 drops green food coloring, or as desired

Decorations:

- 3 (1.75 ounce) packages chocolate sprinkles (jimmies)
- 48 piece (blank)s dark brown candy-coated milk chocolate pieces
- 48 piece (blank)s blue candy-coated milk chocolate pieces
- ⅔ ounce black gel food coloring
- ⅔ ounce red gel food coloring

Directions

Step 1

Preheat oven to 350 degrees F (175 degrees C). Grease or line 12 muffin cups with paper liners.

Step 2

Mix cake mix, water, eggs, and vegetable oil together in a bowl; beat with an electric mixer until batter is smooth, about 2 minutes. Fill muffin cups with batter.

Step 3

Bake in the preheated oven until a toothpick inserted in the center comes out clean, 19 to 23 minutes. Cool cupcakes in the pan for 10 minutes before transferring to a wire rack to cool.

Step 4

Beat shortening and butter together in a bowl using an electric mixer until smooth; add vanilla extract and mix well. Beat confectioners' sugar, alternating with milk, into butter-shortening mixture until frosting is stiff and holds its shape; mix in green food coloring until desired color is reached.

Step 5

Fill a piping bag, or large resealable freezer bag with a corner snipped, with frosting. Pipe frosting around the top half perimeter and top of each cupcake creating the "head" and "face"; smooth out the frosting using a small spatula, flattening the top into a square-shape for the top of his "head."

Step 6

Pour chocolate sprinkles into a shallow bowl and dip the top of each cupcake into the sprinkles, slightly angling the cupcake to get sprinkles around the uppermost top side of the "head" for the "hair."

Step 7

Press 2 dark brown chocolate pieces on the sides of each cupcake creating the "bolts." Press 2 blue chocolate pieces into the top front of each cupcake creating the "eyes." Put a dot of black food gel in the center of each blue candy for the "pupil." Make a "stitch" onto the "face" using the red food gel.

Nutrition Facts

Per Serving:

460.1 calories; protein 2g 4% DV; carbohydrates 60.9g 20% DV; fat 24g 37% DV; cholesterol 44.7mg 15% DV; sodium 186.4mg 8% DV.

Pumpkin Cheesecake Cupcakes

Prep: 25 mins **Cook:** 15 mins **Additional:** 30 mins **Total:** 1 hr 10 mins **Servings:** 24 **Yield:** 24 cupcakes

Ingredients

Crust:

- 1 (4.8 ounce) package graham crackers
- 2 tablespoons ground ginger
- 6 tablespoons butter, melted

Filling:

- 3 (8 ounce) packages cream cheese, softened
- ½ cup white sugar

- ½ cup packed brown sugar
- 1 (15 ounce) can pumpkin puree
- 1 tablespoon ground cinnamon
- 1 tablespoon ground ginger
- 2 teaspoons ground nutmeg
- 1 teaspoon ground cloves
- ¼ teaspoon salt
- 3 large eggs eggs

Topping:

- 1 cup sour cream
- 3 tablespoons confectioners' sugar, or to taste
- 1 tablespoon vanilla extract
- 1 pinch ground cinnamon, for garnish

Directions

Step 1

Preheat oven to 350 degrees F (175 degrees C). Line 24 muffin cups with foil liners.

Step 2

Crush graham crackers and 2 tablespoons ground ginger together in a resealable plastic bag; pour into a bowl. Add butter to graham cracker mixture and mix with a fork or pastry blender until blended.

Step 3

Beat cream cheese, white sugar, and brown sugar together in a large bowl until creamy; beat in pumpkin puree. Add cinnamon, 1 tablespoon ginger, nutmeg, cloves, and salt; add eggs 1 at a time, beating well after each addition.

Step 4

Press 1 tablespoon graham cracker mixture into the base of each prepared muffin cup, pressing mixture slightly up the sides of the liners. Fill each cup with cream cheese mixture.

Step 5

Bake in the preheated oven until tops are smooth and cupcakes jiggle slightly when moved, about 15 minutes. Cool in the pans for 10 minutes before transferring to a wire rack to cool.

Step 6

Stir sour cream, confectioners' sugar, and vanilla extract together in a bowl until frosting is smooth. Top each cheesecake with the topping and sprinkle with cinnamon.

Nutrition Facts

Per Serving:

226.1 calories; protein 3.9g 8% DV; carbohydrates 17.6g 6% DV; fat 16g 25% DV; cholesterol 65.9mg 22% DV; sodium 220.3mg 9% DV.

Simple 'N' Delicious Chocolate Cake

Prep: 15 mins **Cook:** 35 mins **Additional:** 30 mins **Total:** 1 hr 20 mins **Servings:** 8 **Yield:** 1 8-inch pan

Ingredients

- 1 cup white sugar
- 1.063 cups all-purpose flour
- ½ cup unsweetened cocoa powder
- 1 teaspoon baking soda
- 1 teaspoon salt
- ½ cup butter
- 1 egg
- 1 teaspoon vanilla extract
- 1 cup cold, strong, brewed coffee

Directions

Step 1

Preheat oven to 350 degrees F (175 degrees C). Grease and flour an 8-inch pan (see Editor's Note). Sift together flour, cocoa, baking soda and salt. Set aside.

Step 2

In a medium bowl, cream butter and sugar until light and fluffy. Add egg and vanilla and beat well. Add flour mixture, alternating with coffee. Beat until just incorporated.

Step 3

Bake at 350 degrees F (175 degrees C) for 35 to 45 minutes, or until a toothpick inserted into the cake comes out clean. Allow to cool before frosting.

Nutrition Facts

Per Serving:

282 calories; protein 3.7g 7% DV; carbohydrates 40.7g 13% DV; fat 13g 20% DV; cholesterol 53.8mg 18% DV; sodium 540.6mg 22% DV.

Chocolate Cupcakes with Caramel Frosting

Prep: 20 mins **Cook:** 20 mins **Additional:** 1 hr **Total:** 1 hr 40 mins **Servings:** 15 **Yield:** 15 cupcakes

Ingredients

- 1 cup white sugar
- 2 cups all-purpose flour
- ¼ cup unsweetened cocoa powder
- 2 teaspoons baking soda
- 1 cup water
- 2 tablespoons grape jelly
- 1 cup mayonnaise
- 1 teaspoon vanilla extract
- ¼ cup butter, melted
- ⅓ cup half-and-half cream

- ¾ cup packed brown sugar
- ½ teaspoon vanilla extract
- 1 ¾ cups confectioners' sugar

Directions

Step 1

Preheat oven to 350 degrees F (175 degrees C). Grease 15 muffin cups or line with paper baking cups.

Step 2

In a large bowl, stir together the white sugar, flour, cocoa, and baking soda. Make a well in the center, and pour in the water, grape jelly, mayonnaise, and 1 teaspoon of vanilla. Mix just until blended. Spoon the batter into the prepared cups, dividing evenly.

Step 3

Bake in the preheated oven until the tops spring back when lightly pressed, 20 to 25 minutes. Cool in the pan set over a wire rack. When cool, arrange the cupcakes on a serving platter.

Step 4

Make the frosting while the cupcakes cool. Combine the butter, half-and-half and brown sugar in a medium saucepan. Bring to a boil, stirring frequently. Remove from the heat and stir in the confectioners' sugar and vanilla. Set the pan over a bowl of ice water and whisk or beat with an electric mixer until fluffy. Frost cupcakes when they are completely cool.

Nutrition Facts

Per Serving:

361.6 calories; protein 2.3g 5% DV; carbohydrates 54.7g 18% DV; fat 15.7g 24% DV; cholesterol 15.7mg 5% DV; sodium 279.5mg 11% DV.

Caramel Apple Cupcakes

Prep: 20 mins **Cook:** 25 mins **Additional:** 30 mins **Total:** 1 hr 15 mins **Servings:** 24 **Yield:** 2 dozen cupcakes

Ingredients

- 1 (18.25 ounce) package spice cake mix
- 1 ⅓ cups water
- ⅓ cup vegetable oil
- 3 large eggs eggs
- 1 large Granny Smith apple, cored and chopped
- 35 caramels caramels
- ¼ cup evaporated milk
- ½ cup chopped peanuts
- 24 eaches wooden craft sticks

Directions

Step 1

Preheat oven to 350 degrees F (175 degrees C). Line 24 cupcake cups with paper liners.

Step 2

Place cake mix into a large bowl, and pour in water, vegetable oil, and eggs. With an electric mixer on low speed, beat until moistened and combined, about 30 seconds. Increase mixer speed to medium, and beat for 2 minutes. Stir in the chopped apple, and fill the prepared cupcake cups about 2/3 full.

Step 3

Bake in the preheated oven until lightly browned and a wooden toothpick inserted into the center of a cupcake comes out clean, about 20 minutes. Remove cupcake pans to a wire rack to cool.

Step 4

When cupcakes have cooled, melt the caramels with evaporated milk in a saucepan over low heat, stirring constantly until smooth and combined, about 4 minutes. Spread the caramel icing over the cupcakes, and sprinkle with chopped peanuts. Insert a wooden stick into the center of each cupcake.

Nutrition Facts

Per Serving:

209.1 calories; protein 3.7g 7% DV; carbohydrates 29.2g 9% DV; fat 9.2g 14% DV; cholesterol 25mg 8% DV; sodium 193.3mg 8% DV.

Chocolate-Orange Cupcakes with Pistachio Buttercream

Prep: 20 mins **Cook:** 20 mins **Additional:** 30 mins **Total:** 1 hr 10 mins **Servings:** 12 **Yield:** 1 dozen cupcakes

Ingredients

- 1 teaspoon shortening, or as needed
- 1 teaspoon all-purpose flour, or as needed

Cake:

- 1 ½ cups all-purpose flour, sifted
- 1 cup white sugar
- 3 tablespoons cocoa powder
- 1 teaspoon baking soda
- ¼ teaspoon salt
- 1 cup cold water
- ⅓ cup olive oil
- 2 tablespoons orange juice
- ½ teaspoon vanilla extract
- 1 tablespoon grated orange zest

Icing:

- ½ cup unsalted butter
- ⅔ cup confectioners' sugar, sifted
- 2 tablespoons instant pistachio pudding mix
- 2 tablespoons cold water
- 1 ounce dark chocolate, grated

Directions

Step 1

Preheat oven to 350 degrees F (175 degrees C). Grease 12 muffin cups with shortening using a paper towel and dust with about 1 teaspoon flour or line with paper liners.

Step 2

Combine 1 1/2 cups flour, white sugar, cocoa powder, baking soda, and salt in the bowl of a stand mixer. Beat 1 cup cold water, olive oil, orange juice, and vanilla extract into flour mixture on medium-low speed until batter is just combined, about 2 minutes. Fold orange zest into batter. Pour batter into prepared muffin cups, 2/3-full.

Step 3

Bake in the preheated oven until a toothpick inserted into a cupcake comes out clean, about 20 minutes. Transfer cupcakes to a wire rack to cool completely, about 30 minutes.

Step 4

Beat butter in a bowl using an electric mixer in medium speed until fluffy, about 1 minute. Slowly pour confectioners' sugar into creamed butter and beat until incorporated, about 2 minutes. Beat pudding mix into butter mixture until just combined. Add water, 1 tablespoon at a time, until desired consistency of icing is reached. Ice the cooled cupcakes; garnish with grated chocolate.

Nutrition Facts

Per Serving:

300.6 calories; protein 2.1g 4% DV; carbohydrates 40.4g 13% DV; fat 15.2g 23% DV; cholesterol 20.5mg 7% DV; sodium 189.6mg 8% DV.

Worm Cake

Servings: 24 Yield: 24 cupcakes

Ingredients

- 1 (18.25 ounce) package chocolate cake mix
- 3 cups chocolate cookie crumbs
- 1 (16 ounce) package prepared chocolate frosting
- 1 (16 ounce) package gummi worms

Directions

Step 1

Prepare cake mix according to package directions. Pour batter into cupcake pans and bake as directed on cake mix box. Let cupcakes cool thoroughly before frosting.

Step 2

Spread cupcakes lightly with chocolate icing. Sprinkle cookie crumbs on top.

Step 3

Cut gummi worms in half (as many as you like). Put icing onto cut end of the worms and stick to the top of cupcakes. You can use as few or as many as will fit on each cupcake. Let icing set for 10 minutes and then enjoy.

Nutrition Facts

Per Serving:

299.6 calories; protein 4.2g 8% DV; carbohydrates 54.3g 18% DV; fat 8.7g 13% DV; cholesterol 0.3mg; sodium 296.3mg 12% DV.

Candied Yam Cupcakes

Prep: 20 mins **Cook:** 35 mins **Additional:** 30 mins **Total:** 1 hr 25 mins **Servings:** 24 **Yield:** 24 cupcakes

Ingredients

- 1 pound yams, peeled and cubed
- 4 large eggs eggs
- 1 cup canola oil
- 1 cup white sugar
- 1 teaspoon vanilla extract
- 2 cups all-purpose flour
- 2 teaspoons baking powder
- 1 teaspoon baking soda
- 2 teaspoons ground cinnamon
- 1 teaspoon salt
- 3 ounces cream cheese
- ½ cup butter, softened
- 1 teaspoon vanilla extract
- 2 cups confectioners' sugar

Directions

Step 1

Place a steamer insert into a large saucepan, and fill with water to just below the bottom of the steamer. Cover, and bring the water to a boil over high heat. Add the yams, recover, and steam until very tender, about 15 minutes. Remove yams from steamer and allow to cool slightly.

Step 2

Preheat oven to 350 degrees F (175 degrees C). Line 2-12 cup cupcake tins with paper liners.

Step 3

Place eggs, oil, sugar, vanilla extract, and cooked yams in a large bowl; beat with an electric mixer until light and fluffy. Sift together flour, baking powder, baking soda, cinnamon, and salt. Stir dry ingredients into yam mixture, mixing just until combined. Pour batter into paper liners, filling 2/3 full.

Step 4

Bake in preheated oven until a toothpick inserted in the center of a cupcake comes out clean, 17 to 20 minutes. Cool in pans for 5 minutes, transfer to wire rack to cool completely.

Step 5

Beat together cream cheese and butter until fluffy. Beat in the vanilla extract and confectioners sugar; mix until smooth. Frost cool cupcakes with cream cheese frosting.

Nutrition Facts

Per Serving:

275.6 calories; protein 2.7g 6% DV; carbohydrates 32.4g 11% DV; fat 15.4g 24% DV; cholesterol 45.1mg 15% DV; sodium 241.4mg 10% DV.

Fluffy Pumpkin Spiced Cupcakes

Prep: 15 mins **Cook:** 30 mins **Additional:** 1 hr **Total:** 1 hr 45 mins **Servings:** 24 **Yield:** 2 dozen

Ingredients

- 1 (15 ounce) can pumpkin puree
- 1 ½ cups white sugar
- 1 cup packed brown sugar
- ½ cup butter-flavored shortening
- ½ cup butter, softened
- ¼ cup whole milk
- ¼ cup vegetable oil
- 4 large eggs eggs
- 2 cups cake flour
- ¼ cup dry buttermilk powder
- ¼ cup cornstarch
- 2 teaspoons pumpkin pie spice
- 2 teaspoons baking powder
- 1 teaspoon baking soda
- ¾ teaspoon salt

Directions

Step 1

Preheat oven to 350 degrees F (175 degrees C). Line 24 muffin cups with paper muffin liners.

Step 2

Beat the pumpkin puree, white sugar, brown sugar, shortening, butter, milk, vegetable oil, and eggs together in a large bowl until smooth. Whisk the cake flour, dry buttermilk powder, cornstarch, pumpkin pie spice, baking powder, baking soda, and salt together in another bowl. Add the dry ingredients to the pumpkin mixture, stirring until mixed. Pour batter into the prepared muffin cups, filling each cup about 2/3 full.

Step 3

Bake in the preheated until the center of the cupcakes spring back when touched, about 30 minutes. Cool in the pans for 10 minutes before removing to cool completely on a wire rack.

Nutrition Facts

Per Serving:

249.9 calories; protein 2.8g 6% DV; carbohydrates 34.5g 11% DV; fat 11.7g 18% DV; cholesterol 42.3mg 14% DV; sodium 257.9mg 10% DV.

Pumpkin Cupcakes with Cream Cheese Frosting

Prep: 20 mins **Cook:** 20 mins **Additional:** 1 hr **Total:** 1 hr 40 mins **Servings:** 36 **Yield:** 36 servings

Ingredients

Cupcakes:

- 3 cups baking mix (such as Bisquick)
- 1 (15 ounce) can pumpkin puree
- 1 cup white sugar
- 1 cup brown sugar
- 4 large eggs eggs
- ¼ cup butter, softened
- ¼ cup milk
- 2 teaspoons pumpkin pie spice

Cream Cheese Frosting:

- ½ (8 ounce) package cream cheese, softened
- ½ cup butter, softened
- 4 ½ cups confectioners' sugar, divided
- 2 teaspoons vanilla extract

Directions

Step 1

Preheat oven to 350 degrees F (175 degrees C). Grease or line 36 muffin cups with paper liners.

Step 2

Beat baking mix, pumpkin puree, white sugar, brown sugar, eggs, 1/4 cup butter, milk, and pumpkin pie spice together in a bowl using an electric mixer on low speed until well mixed; spoon into the prepared muffin cups.

Step 3

Bake in the preheated oven until a toothpick inserted in the center comes out clean, 20 to 30 minutes. Cool cupcakes in pan for 5 minutes before transferring to a wire rack to cool completely.

Step 4

Beat cream cheese and 1/2 cup butter together in a bowl using an electric mixer on low speed until smooth and creamy. Beat 2 cups confectioners' sugar and vanilla extract into creamed butter mixture on low speed until well mixed; increase to high speed and beat until fluffy. Gradually pour 2 1/2 cups confectioners' sugar into frosting and beat on medium speed until frosting is thickened.

Step 5

Spoon frosting into a resealable plastic bag and snip 1 corner. Pipe frosting onto the cooled cupcakes.

Nutrition Facts

Per Serving:

197.2 calories; protein 1.9g 4% DV; carbohydrates 32.5g 11% DV; fat 7.1g 11% DV; cholesterol 34.4mg 12% DV; sodium 200.8mg 8% DV.

Monster Chocolate Cupcakes for Halloween

Prep: 45 mins **Cook:** 14 mins **Additional:** 1 hr 5 mins **Total:** 2 hrs 4 mins **Servings:** 12 **Yield:** 12 chocolate cupcakes

Ingredients

Chocolate Cupcakes:

- ½ cup milk
- 1 tablespoon white vinegar
- ½ cup unsalted butter, at room temperature
- 10 tablespoons white sugar
- 2 teaspoons vanilla sugar
- 2 large eggs
- ¾ cup all-purpose flour
- 1 tablespoon all-purpose flour
- ½ cup unsweetened cocoa powder
- ½ teaspoon baking powder
- ¼ teaspoon baking soda
- 1 pinch salt

Cream Cheese Frosting:

- 1 (8 ounce) package cream cheese, softened
- ¼ cup unsalted butter, at room temperature
- 1 teaspoon vanilla extract
- 1 cup confectioners' sugar, sifted
- 2 drops green food coloring
- 24 eaches candy eyeballs

Directions

Step 1

Combine milk and vinegar in a bowl. Let stand until milk curdles, about 5 minutes.

Step 2

Preheat oven to 350 degrees F (175 degrees C). Grease a 12-cup muffin tin or line cups with paper liners.

Step 3

Combine 1/2 cup butter, white sugar, and vanilla sugar in a large bowl; beat with an electric mixer until smooth and creamy. Add eggs one at a time, beating well after each addition.

Step 4

Mix 3/4 cup plus 1 tablespoon flour, cocoa powder, baking powder, baking soda, and salt in a bowl. Alternate adding flour mixture and curdled milk to the creamed butter mixture, mixing until batter is well blended. Spoon batter into the prepared muffin cups, filling each 3/4 full.

Step 5

Bake in the preheated oven until tops spring back when lightly pressed and a toothpick inserted in the center of 1 cupcake comes back clean, about 14 minutes. Cool in the muffin tin for a few minutes, then transfer to a wire rack to cool completely, about 1 hour.

Step 6

Combine cream cheese and 1/4 cup butter in a bowl; beat with an electric mixer until well combined. Mix in vanilla extract. Stir in confectioners' sugar gradually. Color frosting green with a few drops of food coloring.

Step 7

Place green frosting in a pastry bag fitted with a grass tip. Hold the pastry bag at a 90-degree angle 1/8 inch above the surface of a cupcake. Squeeze bag to form green 'fur' by pulling tip up and away when the icing strand is about 1/2 inch high. Repeat to cover cupcake evenly with fur. Add 2 eyes to each cupcake.

Nutrition Facts

Per Serving:

315.5 calories; protein 4.5g 9% DV; carbohydrates 32.1g 10% DV; fat 20g 31% DV; cholesterol 82.9mg 28% DV; sodium 133.4mg 5% DV.

Spiced Spider Cupcakes

Prep: 1 hr **Cook:** 25 mins **Additional:** 2 hrs **Total:** 3 hrs 25 mins **Servings:** 24 **Yield:** 2 dozen cupcakes

Ingredients

Spice Cake:

- 3 cups all-purpose flour
- 2 cups white sugar

- 2 teaspoons baking soda
- 1 teaspoon salt
- 1 teaspoon ground cinnamon
- ½ teaspoon ground cloves
- ½ teaspoon ground nutmeg

- 2 cups water
- ⅔ cup canola oil
- 2 tablespoons distilled white vinegar
- 2 teaspoons vanilla extract

Cream Cheese Frosting:

- 2 (3 ounce) packages cream cheese, softened
- ½ cup butter, softened
- 2 teaspoons vanilla extract
- ¼ teaspoon salt

- ⅛ teaspoon ground cinnamon
- 5 cups sifted confectioners' sugar, or more as needed

Decorations:

- 1 (.68 oz. tube) black decorating gel
- 24 large gumdrop (1" dia)s large spiced gumdrops
- black shoestring licorice

Directions

Step 1

Preheat oven to 350 degrees F (175 degrees C). Line cupcake pans with paper liners.

Step 2

Combine flour, white sugar, baking soda, 1 teaspoon salt, 1 teaspoon cinnamon, cloves, and nutmeg in bowl; whisk to mix. In separate bowl, mix water, canola oil, vinegar, and 2 teaspoons vanilla extract. Pour liquids into dry mixture and stir until smooth. The batter will be very thin.

Step 3

Transfer batter into a measuring cup or pitcher; pour batter into prepared cupcake pans.

Step 4

Bake in preheated oven until tops spring back when gently pressed with a fingertip and a toothpick inserted in the center comes out clean, about 25 minutes. Allow cupcakes to cool completely on a wire rack.

Step 5

Beat cream cheese, butter, 2 teaspoons vanilla extract, 1/4 teaspoon salt, and 1/8 teaspoon cinnamon with an electric mixer until smooth. Gradually mix in confectioners' sugar until frosting is creamy and spreadable. Frost the cooled cupcakes.

Step 6

To decorate cupcakes, use black decorating gel to draw a small circle in the center of each cupcake. Draw a larger circle around the first, and continue making larger circles until the last circle is about 1/4 inch from the edge. There should be about 5 rings on each cupcake. Use a toothpick to draw about 8 lines radiating from the center of the cupcake to the edge, like spokes on a wheel, to make webs.

Step 7

Cut the licorice strings into pieces about 1 1/4 inch long for legs. Poke four licorice legs into both sides of each gumdrop. Use decorating gel to make eyes and a smiley mouth on each gumdrop. Place a gumdrop spider onto each cupcake in the center of the webs.

Nutrition Facts

Per Serving:

402.5 calories; protein 2.3g 5% DV; carbohydrates 70.7g 23% DV; fat 12.7g 20% DV; cholesterol 18mg 6% DV; sodium 302.3mg 12% DV.

Halloween Gingerbread Cupcakes

Prep: 40 mins **Cook:** 20 mins **Additional:** 5 mins **Total:** 1 hr 5 mins **Servings:** 12 **Yield:** 12 cupcakes

Ingredients

Reynolds StayBrite Baking Cups

- 6 tablespoons butter, softened
- ½ cup granulated sugar
- 1 ½ teaspoons baking powder
- 1 teaspoon ground cinnamon
- ¼ teaspoon ground ginger
- ¼ teaspoon baking soda
- ¼ teaspoon salt
- 2 large eggs eggs
- 1 cup milk
- ½ cup molasses
- 1 ¾ cups all-purpose flour
- Orange and black decorating sugar

Cinnamon Vanilla Frosting:

- ⅓ cup butter, softened
- ⅓ cup sour cream
- 1 teaspoon vanilla
- 4 cups powdered sugar
- 1 teaspoon ground cinnamon

Directions

Step 1

Preheat oven to 350 degrees F. Line muffin pans with 12 to 18 Reynolds StayBrite Baking Cups with a black swirl design.

Step 2

Beat butter and sugar together in a large bowl with an electric mixer on medium speed for 30 seconds. Add baking powder, cinnamon, ginger, baking soda, and salt. Beat until combined, scraping down sides of the bowl as necessary. Beat in eggs, one at a time.

Step 3

Whisk together the milk and molasses in a medium bowl. Alternately add flour and milk mixture to the butter mixture, beating on low speed after each addition just until combined. Spoon batter evenly into prepared muffin cups, filling each about three-fourths full.

Step 4

Bake 18 to 20 minutes or until a wooden toothpick inserted near centers comes out clean. Cool in pans on a wire rack for 5 minutes. Carefully remove cupcakes from pans; cool completely on a wire rack.

Step 5

Frost with Cinnamon Vanilla Frosting. Sprinkle colored decorating sugars.

Step 6

Cinnamon Vanilla Frosting: Combine butter, sour cream, and vanilla in a large mixing bowl. Beat with an electric mixer on medium speed for 30 seconds. Gradually beat in powdered sugar and ground cinnamon. Thin with 1 to 2 tablespoons milk, if needed to reach desired consistency.

Nutrition Facts

Per Serving:

436.8 calories; protein 3.9g 8% DV; carbohydrates 76.2g 25% DV; fat 13.8g 21% DV; cholesterol 64.3mg 21% DV; sodium 242.2mg 10% DV.

Pull-Apart Spider Web Cupcakes

Prep: 20 mins **Cook:** 20 mins **Additional:** 40 mins **Total:** 1 hr 20 mins **Servings:** 24 **Yield:** 24 cupcakes

Ingredients

- 1 (18.25 ounce) package white cake mix
- 1 cup water
- ⅓ cup vegetable oil
- 3 large eggs eggs
- 2 (16 ounce) containers prepared fluffy white frosting
- 3 drops orange gel food coloring, or as needed
- 1 (.68 oz. tube) black decorating gel

Directions

Step 1

Preheat oven to 350 degrees F (175 degrees C). Line 24 muffin cups with paper muffin liners.

Step 2

Beat cake mix, water, oil, and eggs in a large bowl with an electric mixer on medium speed until batter is completely smooth, about 2 minutes. Divide batter between prepared muffin cups, filling each about 2/3-full.

Step 3

Bake in the preheated oven until tops spring back when pressed, 19 to 23 minutes. Cool for 10 minutes in the pans before removing to a wire rack to cool completely.

Step 4

Beat frosting and orange food coloring together in a bowl until desired shade and consistency are reached.

Step 5

Arrange cooled cupcakes close together in a solid circle shape on a large platter. Spread frosting over cupcakes to create one large, round frosted surface. Squeeze 1 large dot of black decorating gel in the center of the frosting. Draw concentric circles around the dot about 2 inches apart. Drag a toothpick from the center dot to the outermost circle; repeat 12 times to make the surface appear to be a spider's web.

Nutrition Facts

Per Serving:

284.6 calories; protein 1.7g 4% DV; carbohydrates 42.5g 14% DV; fat 12g 19% DV; cholesterol 23.3mg 8% DV; sodium 232mg 9% DV.

Halloween-Inspired Cupcakes

Prep: 1 hr **Total:** 1 hr **Servings:** 12 **Yield:** 12 cupcakes

Ingredients

- 12 eaches unfrosted cupcakes

Spider Cupcake Decoration:

- ½ cup prepared chocolate frosting
- 8 strips red licorice
- 12 piece (blank)s candy-coated milk chocolate pieces (such as M&M's)

Worm Cupcake Decoration:

- ½ cup prepared chocolate frosting
- ¼ cup chocolate cookie crumbs
- 4 piece (blank)s gummy worm candies

Graveyard Cupcake Decoration:

- 1 cup prepared chocolate frosting
- 4 eaches rectangular or oval sandwich cookies (such as Milano)
- ¼ cup chocolate cookie crumbs

Directions

Step 1

For spider cupcakes: Frost 4 cupcakes with a thin layer of chocolate frosting. Cut each licorice strip into 3 pieces. Poke 6 holes around the sides of each cupcake with a skewer. Insert 1 licorice piece into each hole for the spider legs. Place 2 candy-coated milk chocolate pieces as eyes and one for the nose. Add drops of icing to the eyes to make pupils.

Step 2

For worm cupcakes: Frost 4 cupcakes with a thin layer of chocolate frosting. Sprinkle cookie crumbs on top to resemble dirt. Cut gummy worms in half and brush the cut side with some frosting. Stick onto the cupcakes on either side.

Step 3

For graveyard cupcakes: Frost 4 cupcakes with a thin layer of chocolate frosting. Fill a pastry bag fitted with a small plain tip with remaining chocolate frosting. Write "RIP" or draw a cross on each sandwich cookie. Insert decorated cookies into the cupcake so that they look like tombstones. Sprinkle chocolate cookie crumbs around the cookie tombstones to resemble dirt.

Nutrition Facts

Per Serving:

410.5 calories; protein 3.1g 6% DV; carbohydrates 65.9g 21% DV; fat 16.3g 25% DV; cholesterol 19.7mg 7% DV; sodium 254.7mg 10% DV.

Chocolate-Pumpkin Cupcakes

Prep: 15 mins **Cook:** 20 mins **Additional:** 10 mins **Total:** 45 mins **Servings:** 24 **Yield:** 24 cupcakes

Ingredients

- 2 cups white sugar
- 1 ¾ cups all-purpose flour
- ⅓ cup cocoa powder
- 1 ½ teaspoons baking powder
- 1 ½ teaspoons baking soda
- 1 teaspoon salt
- 2 large eggs eggs
- 1 cup pumpkin puree
- 1 cup milk
- ½ cup canola oil
- 2 teaspoons vanilla extract
- ⅓ cup boiling water

Directions

Step 1

Preheat the oven to 350 degrees F (175 degrees C). Line two 12-cup muffin tins with paper liners.

Step 2

Combine sugar, flour, cocoa powder, baking powder, baking soda, and salt in the bowl of an electric mixer. Mix briefly until combined. Add pumpkin, milk, canola oil, and vanilla extract; mix on medium speed for 2 minutes. Add water and mix until just blended.

Step 3

Spoon batter into the prepared muffin cups, filling each almost all the way to the top.

Step 4

Bake in the preheated oven until a toothpick inserted into the center of a cupcake comes out clean, about 20 minutes. Let cool in trays for about 10 minutes before transferring to wire racks to cool completely.

Nutrition Facts

Per Serving:

157.3 calories; protein 2.1g 4% DV; carbohydrates 25.7g 8% DV; fat 5.6g 9% DV; cholesterol 16.3mg 5% DV; sodium 241.2mg 10% DV.

Halloween Cake

Halloween Buttermilk Bundt Cake

Prep: 15 mins **Cook:** 50 mins **Additional:** 15 mins **Total:** 1 hr 20 mins **Servings:** 8 **Yield:**

8 servings

Ingredients

- 2 tablespoons butter, or as needed
- 2 ¼ cups cake flour
- 1 cup white sugar
- 2 teaspoons baking powder
- 1 cup buttermilk, at room temperature
- ¾ cup butter, at room temperature
- 3 eaches eggs, at room temperature
- 1 teaspoon vanilla extract
- 2 teaspoons orange food coloring powder
- ½ cup cocoa powder
- 1 teaspoon black food coloring powder

Directions

Step 1

Preheat the oven to 350 degrees F (175 degrees C). Grease a fluted tube pan (such as Bundt) with 2 tablespoons butter.

Step 2

Mix flour, sugar, and baking powder in a large bowl. Beat in buttermilk using an electric mixer. Add 3/4 cup butter and beat until fully incorporated. Mix in eggs and vanilla extract until smooth.

Step 3

Pour 1/3 of the batter into a small bowl; mix in orange food coloring. Add cocoa powder and black food coloring to the large bowl. Mix well, scraping down the sides.

Step 4

Pour black batter into the cake pan. Pour orange batter on top. Rap pan against the counter to release any air bubbles.

Step 5

Bake in the preheated oven until a toothpick inserted into the center comes out clean, about 50 minutes. Cool for 15 minutes before removing from the pan.

Nutrition Facts

Per Serving:

470.9 calories; protein 7.7g 15% DV; carbohydrates 61.3g 20% DV; fat 23.1g 36% DV; cholesterol 116mg 39% DV; sodium 322.2mg 13% DV.

Rolled Fondant

Prep: 30 mins **Cook:** 5 mins **Total:** 35 mins **Servings:** 16 **Yield:** 1 - 10 x 4 inch high cake (enough to cover)

Ingredients

- 1 (.25 ounce) package unflavored gelatin
- ¼ cup cold water
- ½ cup glucose syrup
- 1 tablespoon glycerin
- 2 tablespoons shortening
- 1 teaspoon vanilla extract
- 8 cups sifted confectioners' sugar

Directions

Step 1

Combine gelatin and cold water; let stand until thick. Place gelatin mixture in top of double boiler and heat until dissolved.

Step 2

Add glucose and glycerin, mix well. Stir in shortening and just before completely melted, remove from heat and stir in vanilla. Mixture should cool until lukewarm.

Step 3

Place 4 cups confectioners' sugar in a large bowl. Make a well in the center and using a wooden spoon, stir in the lukewarm gelatin mixture. Mix in sugar and add more a little at a time, until stickiness disappears. Knead in remaining sugar. Knead until the fondant is smooth, pliable and does not stick to your hands. If fondant is too soft, add more sugar; if too stiff, add water (a drop at a time). Use fondant immediately or store in airtight container in fridge. When ready to use, bring to room temperature and knead again until soft.

Nutrition Facts

Per Serving:

292.9 calories; protein 0.4g 1% DV; carbohydrates 69.8g 23% DV; fat 1.7g 3% DV; cholesterolmg; sodium 1.7mg.

Chocolate Web Cake

Servings: 12 **Yield:** 1 -4 layer 9 inch round cake

Ingredients

- 1 ⅓ cups all-purpose flour
- 2 teaspoons baking powder
- 1 teaspoon salt
- ¼ teaspoon baking soda
- 1 ½ cups white sugar
- ½ cup shortening
- 1 ¼ cups evaporated milk
- 2 large eggs eggs
- 2 (1 ounce) squares unsweetened chocolate, melted
- 1 ⅓ cups shortening
- 1 ⅓ cups white sugar
- ¾ cup evaporated milk
- 2 teaspoons vanilla extract
- 2 (1 ounce) squares unsweetened chocolate, melted

Directions

Step 1

Preheat oven to 350 degrees F(175 degrees C). Grease two 9 inch round cake pans.

Step 2

Sift flour, baking powder, salt, baking soda and 1 1/2 cups of the white sugar together in a large mixing bowl. Add 1/2 cup of the shortening and 1-1/4 cup of the evaporated milk. Beat at medium speed with an electric mixer for 2 minutes. Beat in the eggs and beat for 2 minutes longer. Spread the batter evenly into the prepared pans. Drizzle 1 square of the melted chocolate in a spiral on top of each cake. Feather lines with a knife to form a web pattern.

Step 3

Bake at 350 degrees F (175 degrees C) for 30 to 40 minutes or until a toothpick inserted in the center comes out clean. Let cakes cool in pans for 10 minutes then remove from pans and let cakes cool completely.

Step 4

To Make Filling: Combine the 2 squares unsweetened melted chocolate, 1 1/3 cups shortening, 1 cup white sugar, 3/4 cup evaporated milk and the vanilla together and beat with an electric mixer until smooth.

Step 5

To Assemble Cake: Cut each cooled cake layer in half horizontally. Spread 1/4 of the filling between each layer making a 4 layer cake with a web design on top. Frost sides with the remaining filling.

Nutrition Facts

Per Serving:

627.6 calories; protein 6.5g 13% DV; carbohydrates 65.2g 21% DV; fat 40.3g 62% DV; cholesterol 43.2mg 14% DV; sodium 360mg 14% DV.

Rick's Special Buttercream Frosting

Prep: 30 mins **Total:** 30 mins **Servings:** 12 **Yield:** 7 cups

Ingredients

- 2 cups shortening
- 8 cups confectioners' sugar
- ½ teaspoon salt
- 2 teaspoons vanilla extract
- 1 cup heavy whipping cream

Directions

Step 1

In a mixing bowl, cream shortening until fluffy. Add sugar, and continue creaming until well blended.

Step 2

Add salt, vanilla, and 6 ounces whipping cream. Blend on low speed until moistened. Add additional 2 ounces whipping cream if necessary. Beat at high speed until frosting is fluffy.

Nutrition Facts

Per Serving:

683.7 calories; protein 0.4g 1% DV; carbohydrates 80.3g 26% DV; fat 41.6g 64% DV; cholesterol 27.2mg 9% DV; sodium 105.3mg 4% DV.

Popcorn Cake II

Prep: 20 mins **Cook:** 5 mins **Additional:** 5 mins **Total:** 30 mins **Servings:** 14 **Yield:** 1 -10 inch bundt cake

Ingredients

- 18 cups popped popcorn
- 1 ½ cups gumdrops
- 1 cup whole peanuts
- 1 (10.5 ounce) package miniature marshmallows
- ½ cup butter

Directions

Step 1

Butter one 10 inch tube or bundt pan.

Step 2

Toss the popcorn with the gumdrops and cashews.

Step 3

Melt the marshmallows with the butter or margarine. Pour over the popcorn mixture and mix well. Press the mixture into the prepared pan. Butter hands before pressing firmly into pan. Chill and remove from pan.

Nutrition Facts

Per Serving:

343.6 calories; protein 3.9g 8% DV; carbohydrates 45g 15% DV; fat 18g 28% DV; cholesterol 17.4mg 6% DV; sodium 222.3mg 9% DV.

Marshmallow Fondant

Prep: 29 mins **Cook:** 1 min **Additional:** 8 hrs **Total:** 8 hrs 30 mins **Servings:** 10 **Yield:** 2 1/4 pounds of fondant

Ingredients

- ¼ cup butter
- 1 (16 ounce) package miniature marshmallows
- ¼ cup water
- 1 teaspoon vanilla extract
- 2 pounds confectioners' sugar, divided

Directions

Step 1

Place the butter in a shallow bowl, and set aside.

Step 2

Place the marshmallows in a large microwave-safe bowl, and microwave on High for 30 seconds to 1 minute to start melting the marshmallows. Carefully stir the water and vanilla extract into the hot marshmallows, and stir until the mixture is smooth. Slowly beat in the confectioners' sugar, a cup at a time, until you have a sticky dough. Reserve 1 cup of powdered sugar for kneading. The dough will be very stiff.

Step 3

Rub your hands thoroughly with butter, and begin kneading the sticky dough. As you knead, the dough will become workable and pliable. Turn the dough out onto a working surface dusted with confectioners' sugar and continue kneading until the fondant is smooth and no longer sticky to the touch, 5 to 10 minutes.

Step 4

Form the fondant into a ball, wrap it tightly in plastic wrap, and refrigerate overnight. To use, allow the fondant to come to room temperature, and roll it out onto a flat surface dusted with confectioners' sugar.

Nutrition Facts

Per Serving:

555.1 calories; proteing; carbohydrates 127.3g 41% DV; fat 4.7g 7% DV; cholesterol 12.2mg 4% DV; sodium 89.8mg 4% DV.

Black Magic Cake

Prep: 15 mins **Cook:** 35 mins **Additional:** 10 mins **Total:** 1 hr **Servings:** 24 **Yield:** 1 - 9x13 inch or 2 - 9 inch round pans

Ingredients

- 1 ¾ cups all-purpose flour
- 2 cups white sugar
- ¾ cup unsweetened cocoa powder
- 2 teaspoons baking soda
- 1 teaspoon baking powder
- 1 teaspoon salt
- 2 large eggs eggs
- 1 cup strong brewed coffee
- 1 cup buttermilk
- ½ cup vegetable oil
- 1 teaspoon vanilla extract

Directions

Step 1

Preheat oven to 350 degrees F (175 degrees C). Grease and flour two 9 inch round cake pans or one 9x13 inch pan.

Step 2

In large bowl combine flour, sugar, cocoa, baking soda, baking powder and salt. Make a well in the center.

Step 3

Add eggs, coffee, buttermilk, oil and vanilla. Beat for 2 minutes on medium speed. Batter will be thin. Pour into prepared pans.

Step 4

Bake at 350 degrees F (175 degrees C) for 30 to 40 minutes, or until toothpick inserted into center of cake comes out clean. Cool for 10 minutes, then remove from pans and finish cooling on a wire rack. Fill and frost as desired.

Nutrition Facts

Per Serving:

155.1 calories; protein 2.3g 5% DV; carbohydrates 25.7g 8% DV; fat 5.5g 9% DV; cholesterol 15.9mg 5% DV; sodium 239.6mg 10% DV.

Pumpkin Cake

Servings: 16 **Yield:** 1 10-inch bundt cake

Ingredients

- 1 cup vegetable oil
- 3 large eggs eggs
- 1 (15 ounce) can pumpkin puree
- 1 teaspoon vanilla extract
- 2 ½ cups white sugar
- 2 ½ cups all-purpose flour
- 1 teaspoon baking soda
- 1 teaspoon ground nutmeg
- 1 teaspoon ground allspice
- 1 teaspoon ground cinnamon
- 1 teaspoon ground cloves
- ¼ teaspoon salt
- ¼ cup chopped nuts

Directions

Step 1

Preheat oven to 350 degrees F (175 degrees C). Grease one 10 inch bundt or tube pan.

Step 2

Cream oil, beaten eggs, pumpkin, and vanilla together.

Step 3

Sift the flour, sugar, baking soda, ground nutmeg, ground allspice, ground cinnamon, ground cloves and salt together. Add the flour mixture to the pumpkin mixture and mix until just combined. If desired, stir in some chopped nuts. Pour batter into the prepared pan.

Step 4

Bake at 350 degrees F (175 degrees C) for 1 hour or until a toothpick inserted in the middle comes out clean. Let cake cool in pan for 5 minutes then turn out onto a plate and sprinkle with confectioners' sugar.

Nutrition Facts

Per Serving:

352.6 calories; protein 3.9g 8% DV; carbohydrates 49.3g 16% DV; fat 16.3g 25% DV; cholesterol 34.9mg 12% DV; sodium 193.4mg 8% DV.

Dirt Cake I

Servings: 10 **Yield:** 1 medium size flower pot

Ingredients

- ½ cup butter, softened
- 1 (8 ounce) package cream cheese, softened
- ½ cup confectioners' sugar
- 2 (3.5 ounce) packages instant vanilla pudding mix
- 3 ½ cups milk
- 1 (12 ounce) container frozen whipped topping, thawed
- 32 ounces chocolate sandwich cookies with creme filling

Directions

Step 1

Chop cookies very fine in food processor. The white cream will disappear.

Step 2

Mix butter, cream cheese, and sugar in bowl.

Step 3

In a large bowl mix milk, pudding and whipped topping together.

Step 4

Combine pudding mixture and cream mixture together.

Step 5

Layer in flower pot, starting with cookies then cream mixture. Repeat layers.

Step 6

Chill until ready to serve.

Step 7

Add artificial flower and trowel. Enjoy!

Nutrition Facts

Per Serving:

827.3 calories; protein 9.9g 20% DV; carbohydrates 101.5g 33% DV; fat 44.6g 69% DV; cholesterol 55.9mg 19% DV; sodium 895.8mg 36% DV.

Pumpkin Cake III

Prep: 30 mins **Cook:** 30 mins **Total:** 1 hr **Servings:** 14 **Yield:** 1 - 12x18 inch pan

Ingredients

- 2 cups white sugar
- 1 ¼ cups vegetable oil
- 1 teaspoon vanilla extract
- 2 cups canned pumpkin
- 4 large eggs eggs
- 2 cups all-purpose flour
- 3 teaspoons baking powder
- 2 teaspoons baking soda
- ¼ teaspoon salt
- 2 teaspoons ground cinnamon
- 1 cup chopped walnuts

Directions

Step 1

Preheat oven to 350 degrees F (175 degrees C). Grease and flour a 12x18 inch pan. Sift together the flour, baking powder, baking soda, salt and cinnamon. Set aside.

Step 2

In a large bowl combine sugar and oil. Blend in vanilla and pumpkin, then beat in eggs one at a time. Gradually beat in flour mixture. Stir in nuts. Spread batter into prepared 12x18 inch pan.

Step 3

Bake in the preheated oven for 30 minutes, or until a toothpick inserted into the center of the cake comes out clean. Allow to cool.

Nutrition Facts

Per Serving:

438.4 calories; protein 5.3g 11% DV; carbohydrates 46.8g 15% DV; fat 26.8g 41% DV; cholesterol 53.1mg 18% DV; sodium 404.1mg 16% DV.

Great Pumpkin Dessert

Servings: 24 **Yield:** 1 - 9x13 inch pan

Ingredients

- 1 (15 ounce) can pumpkin puree
- 1 (12 fluid ounce) can evaporated milk
- 3 large eggs eggs
- 1 cup white sugar
- 4 teaspoons pumpkin pie spice
- 1 (18.25 ounce) package yellow cake mix
- ¾ cup butter, melted
- 1 ½ cups chopped walnuts

Directions

Step 1

Preheat oven to 350 degrees F (175 degrees C). Grease a 9x13 inch baking pan.

Step 2

In a large bowl, combine pumpkin, milk, eggs, sugar and spice. Mix well, and pour into a 9x13 inch pan.

Step 3

Sprinkle dry cake mix over the top, then drizzle with melted butter. Top with walnuts.

Step 4

Bake at 350 degrees F (175 degrees C) for 1 hour or until a knife inserted near the center comes out clean.

Nutrition Facts

Per Serving:

261 calories; protein 4.2g 8% DV; carbohydrates 29.4g 10% DV; fat 14.9g 23% DV; cholesterol 43.5mg 15% DV; sodium 250.9mg 10% DV.

Pumpkin Squares

Servings: 24 **Yield:** 1 9x13 inch pan.

Ingredients

- 4 large eggs eggs
- 1 cup vegetable oil
- 2 cups white sugar
- 1 (15 ounce) can solid pack pumpkin puree
- 2 cups all-purpose flour
- 2 teaspoons ground cinnamon
- ½ teaspoon ground cloves
- ½ teaspoon ground ginger
- ½ teaspoon ground nutmeg
- 1 teaspoon baking soda
- 2 teaspoons baking powder
- ½ teaspoon salt

Directions

Step 1

Preheat oven to 350 degrees F (175 degrees C). Grease a 9x13 inch baking pan.

Step 2

In a medium bowl, mix together the eggs, oil, sugar and pumpkin until smooth. Sift together the flour, cinnamon, cloves, ginger, nutmeg, baking soda, baking powder and salt. Stir into the pumpkin mixture.

Step 3

Spread evenly into the prepared pan and bake for 25 to 30 minutes. The bars should spring back to the touch when done. Allow to cool before frosting.

Nutrition Facts

Per Serving:

202.7 calories; protein 2.3g 5% DV; carbohydrates 26.5g 9% DV; fat 10.2g 16% DV; cholesterol 31mg 10% DV; sodium 196.3mg 8% DV.

Graveyard Cake for Halloween

Prep: 30 mins **Cook:** 26 mins **Additional:** 2 hrs 15 mins **Total:** 3 hrs 11 mins **Servings:** 16

Yield: 16 servings

Ingredients

- cooking spray
- 1 (15.25 ounce) package chocolate cake mix (such as Duncan Hines)
- 1 cup water
- 3 eaches eggs
- ⅓ cup vegetable oil
- 1 (16 ounce) package prepared chocolate frosting
- 15 eaches rectangular or oval sandwich cookies (such as Milano)
- 10 eaches chocolate wafer cookies, crushed

Directions

Step 1

Preheat oven to 350 degrees F (175 degrees C). Grease sides and bottom of a 9x13-inch cake pan with cooking spray.

Step 2

Combine cake mix, water, eggs, and oil in a large bowl; beat with an electric mixer on low speed until moistened, about 30 seconds. Beat at medium speed until batter is smooth and creamy, about 2 minutes. Pour batter into the prepared pan.

Step 3

Bake in the preheated oven until a toothpick inserted in the center comes out clean, 26 to 31 minutes. Remove from oven and cool pan on wire rack for 15 minutes. Remove cake from pan and cool completely on wire rack before decorating, about 2 hours.

Step 4

Spread a layer of chocolate frosting over top of the cake.

Step 5

Fill a pastry bag, fitted with a small plain tip, with a few tablespoons of chocolate frosting. Write "RIP" or draw a cross on sandwich cookies. Insert decorated cookies into the cake so that they look like tombstones in a graveyard. Sprinkle chocolate cookie crumbs in between the cookie tombstones to resemble dirt.

Nutrition Facts

Per Serving:

338.6 calories; protein 3.6g 7% DV; carbohydrates 44.6g 14% DV; fat 17.8g 27% DV; cholesterol 33.8mg 11% DV; sodium 312.8mg 13% DV.

Grandma Carol's Pumpkin Roll

Prep: 30 mins **Cook:** 10 mins **Additional:** 1 hr 10 mins **Total:** 1 hr 50 mins **Servings:** 24

Yield: 1 cake

Ingredients

- 3 large eggs eggs, beaten
- 1 cup white sugar
- ⅔ cup pumpkin puree
- ¾ cup all-purpose flour
- 1 teaspoon baking soda
- 1 teaspoon ground cinnamon
- ½ teaspoon ground cloves
- ½ teaspoon ground nutmeg
- 1 (8 ounce) package cream cheese, softened

- 2 tablespoons butter
- 1 (16 ounce) package confectioners' sugar
- 1 teaspoon vanilla extract

- 1 cup chopped pecans
- 2 teaspoons confectioners' sugar for dusting, or as needed

Directions

Step 1

Preheat oven to 400 degrees F (200 degrees C). Butter a 12x17-inch jelly roll pan and line with parchment paper; butter the parchment paper. Generously dust a kitchen towel with confectioners' sugar.

Step 2

Beat eggs, white sugar, and pumpkin together in a bowl until creamy.

Step 3

Sift flour, baking soda, cinnamon, cloves, and nutmeg together in a separate bowl; gradually stir into egg mixture. Stir to combine. Spread batter evenly into the prepared pan.

Step 4

Bake in the preheated oven for exactly 10 minutes.

Step 5

Immediately turn cake onto the prepared kitchen towel. Starting at a long end, roll up pumpkin cake and towel. Let rolled cake rest for 10 minutes.

Step 6

Beat cream cheese, butter, 16-ounce package confectioners' sugar, and vanilla extract together in a bowl until smooth; fold in pecans.

Step 7

Unroll cake; spread with the filling. Roll up cake (without towel). Cut off any jagged ends. Cover and refrigerate until chilled. Cut cake in half if desired; sprinkle with confectioners' sugar before serving.

Cake Pops

Prep: 30 mins **Cook:** 10 mins **Additional:** 1 hr **Total:** 1 hr 40 mins **Servings:** 24 **Yield:**

24 pops

Ingredients

- 1 (12 ounce) package colored candy coating melts, divided
- 24 doughnut holes plain doughnut holes
- 24 eaches lollipop sticks
- 1 tablespoon multicolored candy sprinkles (jimmies), as desired

Directions

Step 1

Place about 1/4 cup of candy melts into a small microwave-safe bowl, and melt in the microwave at 40 percent power for 30 seconds; stir the candy coating, and continue to heat for 30 second-intervals until the coating is just warm and completely melted.

Step 2

Poke a hole halfway through a doughnut hole with a lollipop stick, then dip the end of the stick into the melted coating and reinsert into the hole. This holds the doughnut hole firmly on the stick. Stick the doughnut pop upright into a block of plastic foam, and set into refrigerator for 1 hour to firm up.

Step 3

When pops are firmly attached to their sticks, melt the remaining candy coating dots in a microwave-safe bowl on 40 percent power for 1 minute; stir, and melt for 30-second intervals until the coating is warm and smoothly melted. Dip the doughnut hole into the coating, covering it completely. Hold the dipped pop over a bowl, and sprinkle with colored candy sprinkles. Return the decorated pops to the plastic foam block to set.

Nutrition Facts

Per Serving:

131.3 calories; protein 1.7g 3% DV; carbohydrates 14.5g 5% DV; fat 7.6g 12% DV; cholesterol 3.8mg 1% DV; sodium 57.3mg 2% DV.

Pumpkin Roll with Ginger and Pecans

Prep: 35 mins **Cook:** 20 mins **Additional:** 1 day **Total:** 1 day **Servings:** 15 **Yield:** 1 pumpkin roll

Ingredients

- 3 large eggs eggs
- 1 cup white sugar
- ⅔ cup solid pack pumpkin puree
- 1 teaspoon lemon juice
- ¾ cup all-purpose flour
- 1 teaspoon baking powder
- ½ teaspoon salt
- 2 teaspoons ground cinnamon

- 1 teaspoon ground ginger
- 1 cup chopped pecans
- confectioners' sugar for dusting
- 1 (8 ounce) package cream cheese
- 4 tablespoons butter
- 1 cup confectioners' sugar
- ½ teaspoon vanilla extract
- confectioners' sugar for dusting

Directions

Step 1

Preheat oven to 350 degrees F (175 degrees C). Grease and flour a 10x15 inch jellyroll pan.

Step 2

In a large bowl, beat eggs and sugar with an electric mixer on high speed for five minutes. Gradually mix in pumpkin and lemon juice. Combine the flour, baking powder, salt, cinnamon, and ginger; stir into the pumpkin mixture. Spread batter evenly into the prepared pan. Sprinkle pecans over the top of the batter.

Step 3

Bake for 12 to 15 minutes, or until the center springs back when touched. Loosen edges with a knife. Turn out on two dishtowels that have been dusted with confectioners' sugar. Roll up cake using towels, and let cool for about 20 minutes.

Step 4

In a medium bowl, combine cream cheese, butter, 1 cup confectioners' sugar, and vanilla. Beat until smooth. Unroll pumpkin cake when cool, spread with filling, and roll up. Place pumpkin roll on a long sheet of waxed paper, and dust with confectioners' sugar. Wrap cake in waxed paper, and twist ends of waxed paper like a candy wrapper. Refrigerate overnight. Serve chilled; before slicing, dust with additional confectioners' sugar.

Nutrition Facts

Per Serving:

279.2 calories; protein 3.9g 8% DV; carbohydrates 35.1g 11% DV; fat 14.6g 23% DV; cholesterol 61.8mg 21% DV; sodium 216.6mg 9% DV.

Nickie's Apple-Pecan Cheesecake

Prep: 30 mins **Cook:** 55 mins **Additional:** 4 hrs 30 mins **Total:** 5 hrs 55 mins **Servings:** 16
Yield: 16 servings

Ingredients

Crust

- 1 ½ cups graham cracker crumbs
- ¼ cup melted butter
- 2 tablespoons packed brown sugar

Filling

- 4 (8 ounce) packages cream cheese, softened
- 1 cup packed brown sugar
- 1 teaspoon vanilla extract
- 1 cup sour cream
- 4 large eggs eggs

Topping

- 4 cups apples (about 3) - peeled, cored, and chopped
- ½ cup packed brown sugar
- ¾ cup chopped pecans
- 1 teaspoon ground cinnamon

Directions

Step 1

Preheat oven to 325 degrees F (165 degrees C). Line a 9x13 inch baking dish with aluminum foil, extending the foil sheets over the side of the dish.

Step 2

To make the crust, mix the graham cracker crumbs, butter, and 2 tablespoons brown sugar together in a bowl until evenly blended. Press evenly over the bottom of the prepared baking dish.

Step 3

To make the filling, beat the cream cheese, 1 cup brown sugar, and vanilla together in a mixing bowl until evenly blended. Beat in the sour cream. On low speed, add the eggs, one at a time, just until blended. Pour the mixture over the crust.

Step 4

To make the topping, place the apples in a bowl, and toss with 1/2 cup brown sugar, pecans, and cinnamon until evenly blended.

Step 5

Bake in preheated oven until center is almost set, about 55 minutes. Cool, and refrigerate 4 hours, or overnight.

Step 6

Before cutting, allow the cheesecake to sit 30 minutes at room temperature, then lift from the baking dish using the extended aluminum foil sheets, and place on a cutting board or serving plate. Remove the aluminum foil, and cut into 16 squares.

Pumpkin Pie No-Bake Cheesecake

Prep: 20 mins **Additional:** 3 hrs 15 mins **Total:** 3 hrs 35 mins **Servings:** 8 **Yield:** 8 servings

Ingredients

- 1 (8 ounce) package low-fat cream cheese
- ⅓ cup white sugar
- 1 ½ tablespoons lemon juice
- 1 ½ teaspoons vanilla extract
- 1 (15 ounce) can pumpkin puree, divided
- 1 teaspoon ground cinnamon
- ½ teaspoon ground ginger
- ½ teaspoon ground nutmeg
- ½ cup heavy whipping cream
- 1 (9 inch) prepared graham cracker crust

Directions

Step 1

Place a bowl and beaters for a hand-held electric mixer into the freezer to cool, about 15 minutes.

Step 2

Mix cream cheese and sugar together in a bowl; stir in lemon juice and vanilla extract. Fold in half of the pumpkin puree; add cinnamon, ginger, and nutmeg.

Step 3

Remove the bowl and beaters from the freezer. Attach beaters to an electric mixer; pour cream into chilled bowl. Beat until stiff peaks form and cream stays in place when the bowl is tipped on its side.

Step 4

Fold remaining pumpkin puree and whipped cream into the cream cheese mixture. Spread evenly into crust; cover with plastic wrap.

Step 5

Chill in the refrigerator until set, 3 to 4 hours.

Nutrition Facts

Per Serving:

320 calories; protein 5.2g 10% DV; carbohydrates 35.3g 11% DV; fat 18.2g 28% DV; cholesterol 36.3mg 12% DV; sodium 388.8mg 16% DV.

Chocolate Buttermilk Layer Cake

Prep: 30 mins **Cook:** 20 mins **Additional:** 45 mins **Total:** 1 hr 35 mins **Servings:** 12

Yield: 12 servings

Ingredients

- ¾ cup NESTLE TOLL HOUSE Baking Cocoa, plus extra for coating pans
- 2 ¼ cups cake flour
- 2 teaspoons baking soda
- 1 teaspoon fine salt
- 1 ¼ cups buttermilk, at room temperature
- ½ cup brewed coffee or water
- 2 teaspoons vanilla extract
- 1 cup unsalted butter, at room temperature
- 2 cups superfine sugar
- 4 large eggs, at room temperature
- 2 (16 ounce) containers prepared chocolate frosting, or more if needed
- 1 (1.55 ounce) bar NESTLE CRUNCH Candy Bars, finely chopped (or more if needed)
- 24 pieces NESTLE BUTTERFINGER Bites Candy, finely chopped (or more if needed)

Directions

Step 1

Preheat oven to 350 degrees F. Grease bottoms of three 8- or 9-inch-round cake pans; line with a parchment or wax paper circle. Grease parchment, then coat lightly with small amount of cocoa, tapping out excess.

Step 2

Sift flour, cup cocoa, baking soda and salt together into a large bowl. Combine buttermilk, coffee and vanilla extract in small bowl.

Step 3

Beat butter in large mixer bowl until smooth. Beat in sugar until smooth and creamy. Beat in eggs one at a time, beating well after each addition. Scrape down sides of bowl with rubber spatula; beat again. Alternately add flour mixture in three additions with the buttermilk mixture in two additions, beginning and ending with flour mixture. Scrape down sides of bowl; beat again. Pour batter evenly into prepared pans.

Step 4

Bake for 20 to 25 minutes or until wooden pick inserted in center comes out clean. Cool in pans on wire racks for 10 minutes. Invert each layer onto wire rack; remove parchment paper, then invert right-side-up. Cool completely.

Step 5

To assemble: Level (trim tops off) the cakes if desired using a serrated knife. Place a dollop of frosting in the center of a cake pedestal or serving platter so the cake won't slip. Tear four strips of parchment paper and place in a square around the outer 3 inches of pedestal (this will help prevent getting the frosting on the pedestal). Place one cake layer over dollop of frosting. Spread about 1 cup frosting over top; sprinkle top evenly with about 1/4 cup chopped Crunch bar. Top with another cake layer; spread with about 1 cup frosting. Sprinkle with remaining chopped Crunch bar. Top with third cake layer. Cover the top and sides with a thin layer of frosting (this is the "crumb coat"; it doesn't have to be perfect). Refrigerate for 15 minutes, then cover with the remaining frosting. With hands, press chopped Butterfinger around sides of cake. After the frosting has set, gently remove strips of parchment paper. Cut cake into slices for serving.

Nutrition Facts

Per Serving:

805.4 calories; protein 6.9g 14% DV; carbohydrates 108.1g 35% DV; fat 38.5g 59% DV; cholesterol 103.7mg 35% DV; sodium 701.4mg 28% DV.

Pumpkin Patch "Dirt" Cake

Prep: 30 mins **Additional:** 1 hr **Total:** 1 hr 30 mins **Servings:** 12 **Yield:** 12 servings

Ingredients

- 1 (19.1 ounce) package chocolate sandwich cookies (such as Oreo)
- 2 (24 ounce) round cartons chocolate ice cream
- ½ cup prepared vanilla frosting
- 1 drop green food coloring
- 30 eaches mellocreme (candy corn) pumpkins

Directions

Step 1

Crush the cookies in 2 batches in a food processor. You'll need about 4 1/3 cups crumbs.

Step 2

Spread 1 1/3 cups crumbs over bottom of a 9-x-13-inch baking pan.

Step 3

Cut away cardboard packaging from 1 carton of ice cream with scissors. Slice ice cream crosswise into 1-inch-thick rounds with a long knife. Arrange slices over crumbs, cutting smaller pieces to fill gaps. Cover ice cream with another 1 1/3 cups crumbs. Repeat with second container of ice cream, and top with remaining crumbs. Freeze until firm, at least 1 hour.

Step 4

Mix frosting with enough green food coloring to make it bright green, then transfer to a pastry bag fitted with a plain tip. Arrange 3 double rows of pumpkins on top of cake and pipe vines connecting pumpkins. Freeze until ready to serve.

Nutrition Facts

Per Serving:

541 calories; protein 6.7g 13% DV; carbohydrates 82.3g 27% DV; fat 22.6g 35% DV; cholesterol 38.6mg 13% DV; sodium 322.8mg 13% DV.

Kitty Litter Cake

Servings: 20 **Yield:** 20 servings

Ingredients

- 1 (18.25 ounce) package German chocolate cake mix
- 1 (18.25 ounce) package white cake mix
- 2 (3.5 ounce) packages instant vanilla pudding mix
- 1 (12 ounce) package vanilla sandwich cookies
- 3 drops green food coloring
- 1 (12 ounce) package tootsie rolls

Directions

Step 1

Prepare cake mixes and bake according to package directions (any size pan).

Step 2

Prepare pudding according to package directions and chill until ready to assemble.

Step 3

Crumble sandwich cookies in small batches in a food processor, scraping often. Set aside all but 1/4 cup. To the 1/4 cup add a few drops of green food coloring and mix.

Step 4

When cakes are cooled to room temperature, crumble them into a large bowl. Toss with 1/2 of the remaining cookie crumbs, and the chilled pudding. You probably won't need all of the pudding, you want the cake to be just moist, not soggy.

Step 5

Line kitty litter box with the kitty litter liner. Put cake mixture into box.

Step 6

Put half of the unwrapped tootsie rolls in a microwave safe dish and heat until softened. Shape the ends so that they are no longer blunt, and curve the tootsie rolls slightly. Bury tootsie rolls randomly in the cake and sprinkle with half of the remaining cookie crumbs. Sprinkle a small amount of the green colored cookie crumbs lightly over the top.

Step 7

Heat 3 or 4 of the tootsie rolls in the microwave until almost melted. Scrape them on top of the cake and sprinkle lightly with some of the green cookie crumbs. Heat the remaining tootsie rolls until pliable and shape as before. Spread all but one randomly over top of cake mixture. Sprinkle with any remaining cookie crumbs. Hang the remaining tootsie roll over side of litter box and sprinkle with a few green cookie crumbs. Serve with the pooper scooper for a gross Halloween dessert.

Nutrition Facts

Per Serving:

351.2 calories; protein 3.4g 7% DV; carbohydrates 76.6g 25% DV; fat 7.5g 12% DV; cholesterolmg; sodium 592.9mg 24% DV.

Granny Kat's Pumpkin Roll

Prep: 20 mins **Cook:** 15 mins **Additional:** 20 mins **Total:** 55 mins **Servings:** 10 **Yield:** 10 servings

Ingredients

- ¾ cup all-purpose flour
- 1 cup white sugar
- 1 teaspoon baking soda
- 2 teaspoons pumpkin pie spice
- 1 cup pumpkin puree
- 3 large eggs eggs
- 1 teaspoon lemon juice
- 2 tablespoons confectioners' sugar
- 1 (8 ounce) package cream cheese, softened
- ¼ cup butter
- 1 teaspoon vanilla extract
- 1 cup confectioners' sugar

Directions

Step 1

Preheat oven to 375 degrees F (190 degrees C). Grease and flour a 9x13 inch jelly roll pan or cookie sheet.

Step 2

In a large bowl, mix together flour, sugar, baking soda, and pumpkin pie spice. Stir in pumpkin puree, eggs, and lemon juice. Pour mixture into prepared pan. Spread the mixture evenly.

Step 3

Bake at 375 degrees F (190 degrees C) for 15 minutes.

Step 4

Lay a damp linen towel on the counter, sprinkle it with confectioner's sugar, and turn the cake onto the towel. Carefully roll the towel up (lengthwise) with the cake in it. Place the cake-in-towel on a cooling rack and let it cool for 20 minutes.

Step 5

Make the icing: In a medium bowl, blend cream cheese, butter, vanilla, and sugar with a wooden spoon or electric mixer.

Step 6

When the cake has cooled 20 minutes, unroll it and spread icing onto it. Immediately re-roll (not in the towel this time), and wrap it with plastic wrap. Keep the cake refrigerated or freeze it for up to 2 weeks in aluminum foil. Cut the cake in slices just before serving.

Nutrition Facts

Per Serving:

315.6 calories; protein 4.9g 10% DV; carbohydrates 43.7g 14% DV; fat 14.1g 22% DV; cholesterol 92.6mg 31% DV; sodium 305.5mg 12% DV.

Chocolate Candy Bar Cake

Prep: 45 mins **Cook:** 25 mins **Total:** 1 hr 10 mins **Servings:** 12 **Yield:** 3 layer 8 inch cake

Ingredients

- 1 (18.25 ounce) package devil's food cake mix
- 1 ½ cups milk
- 3 large eggs eggs

- ¾ cup vegetable oil
- 1 (3.5 ounce) package instant vanilla pudding mix
- 1 (8 ounce) package cream cheese
- ½ cup white sugar
- 1 cup confectioners' sugar
- 1 (12 ounce) container frozen whipped topping, thawed
- 1 cup chopped pecans
- 4 (1.5 ounce) bars milk chocolate candy, coarsely chopped

Directions

Step 1

Preheat oven to 325 degrees F (165 degrees C). Grease and flour 3 (8 inch) pans.

Step 2

In a large bowl, combine cake mix, milk, eggs, oil and instant vanilla pudding mix. Beat on low speed until blended. Scrape bowl, and beat 4 minutes on medium speed. Pour batter into prepared pans.

Step 3

Bake in the preheated oven for 20 to 25 minutes, or until a toothpick inserted into the center of the cake comes out clean. Allow to cool.

Step 4

To make the frosting: In a large bowl, beat the cream cheese with the white sugar and confectioners' sugar until smooth. Fold in the whipped topping, pecans and chopped chocolate. Spread between layers and on top and sides of cake.

Nutrition Facts

Per Serving:

735.8 calories; protein 9.3g 19% DV; carbohydrates 75.2g 24% DV; fat 46.1g 71% DV; cholesterol 81.4mg 27% DV; sodium 535.4mg 21% DV.

Pumpkin Sheet Cake

Prep: 30 mins **Cook:** 30 mins **Additional:** 1 hr **Total:** 2 hrs **Servings:** 20 **Yield:** 1 - 10 x 15 inch cake

Ingredients

- 1 (15 ounce) can canned pumpkin puree
- 2 cups white sugar
- 1 cup vegetable oil
- 4 large eggs eggs
- 2 cups all-purpose flour
- 2 teaspoons baking soda
- 1 teaspoon ground cinnamon
- ½ teaspoon salt
- 1 (3 ounce) package cream cheese
- 5 tablespoons butter, softened
- 1 teaspoon vanilla extract
- 1 ¾ cups confectioners' sugar
- 3 teaspoons milk
- 1 cup chopped walnuts

Directions

Step 1

In a mixing bowl, beat pumpkin, 2 cups white sugar, and oil. Add eggs, and mix well.

Step 2

In another bowl, combine flour, baking soda, cinnamon and salt. Add these dry ingredients to the pumpkin mixture, and beat until well blended. Pour batter into a greased 15 x 10 inch baking pan.

Step 3

Bake at 350 degrees F (175 degrees C) for 25 to 30 minutes, or until cake tests done. Cool.

Step 4

In a mixing bowl, beat the cream cheese, butter or margarine, and vanilla until smooth. Gradually add 1 3/4 cups confectioners' sugar, and mix well. Add milk until frosting reaches desired spreading consistency. Frost cake, and sprinkle with nuts.

Nutrition Facts

Per Serving:

362 calories; protein 4g 8% DV; carbohydrates 42.8g 14% DV; fat 20.4g 31% DV; cholesterol 49.5mg 17% DV; sodium 282.9mg 11% DV.

Cream Cheese Pumpkin Roll

Prep: 25 mins **Cook:** 15 mins **Additional:** 2 hrs 10 mins **Total:** 2 hrs 50 mins **Servings:** 10

Yield: 1 roll

Ingredients

- 3 large eggs eggs
- 1 cup white sugar
- ⅔ cup pumpkin puree
- ¾ cup all-purpose flour
- 2 teaspoons ground cinnamon

- 1 teaspoon baking powder
- 1 teaspoon ground ginger
- ½ teaspoon ground nutmeg
- ½ teaspoon salt

Filling:

- 1 (8 ounce) package cream cheese, softened
- 1 cup confectioners' sugar

- ¼ cup butter, softened
- 1 tablespoon pumpkin puree
- 1 teaspoon vanilla extract

Directions

Step 1

Preheat oven to 375 degrees F (190 degrees C). Grease a 10x15-inch jelly roll pan and line with wax paper.

Step 2

Beat eggs and white sugar in a large bowl until well blended; stir in 2/3 cup pumpkin puree.

Step 3

Combine flour, cinnamon, baking powder, ginger, nutmeg, and salt in another bowl; stir into egg mixture until just blended. Pour mixture into prepared jelly roll pan.

Step 4

Bake in preheated oven until a toothpick inserted into the center comes out clean, about 15 minutes. Cool in the pans for 10 minutes, then turn cake out onto a clean towel. Remove and discard wax paper. Roll cake up into the towel, starting with the short end. Cool.

Step 5

Beat cream cheese, confectioners' sugar, butter, 1 tablespoon pumpkin puree, and vanilla extract in another bowl until smooth.

Step 6

Spread a large sheet of plastic wrap on a work surface. Place and unroll cake over plastic and spread with prepared filling. Re-roll cake and wrap with plastic. Refrigerate, seam-side down, until chilled, about 2 hours.

Nutrition Facts

Per Serving:

308.1 calories; protein 4.8g 10% DV; carbohydrates 41.9g 14% DV; fat 14.1g 22% DV; cholesterol 92.6mg 31% DV; sodium 324.9mg 13% DV.

Pumpkin Spiced Dump Cake

Prep: 10 mins **Cook:** 1 hr **Total:** 1 hr 10 mins **Servings:** 12 **Yield:** 12 servings

Ingredients

- cooking spray
- 1 (15 ounce) can pumpkin puree
- 1 (12 fluid ounce) can evaporated milk
- 1 ½ cups white sugar
- 4 large eggs eggs
- 1 teaspoon vanilla extract
- ½ teaspoon ground cinnamon
- ¼ teaspoon ground nutmeg
- 1 (15.25 ounce) package yellow cake mix
- 2 cups chopped pecans
- ¾ cup butter, melted

Directions

Step 1

Preheat oven to 325 degrees F (165 degrees C). Grease a 9x13-inch baking pan with cooking spray.

Step 2

Mix pumpkin, evaporated milk, sugar, eggs, vanilla extract, cinnamon, and nutmeg together in a bowl; pour into the prepared baking pan.

Step 3

Sprinkle cake mix evenly over the pumpkin mixture; top with pecans. Drizzle melted butter on top.

Step 4

Bake in the preheated oven until golden brown, about 1 hour.

Nutrition Facts

Per Serving:

571 calories; protein 8.2g 16% DV; carbohydrates 62.2g 20% DV; fat 34.1g 53% DV; cholesterol 102.4mg 34% DV; sodium 460.6mg 18% DV.

Pumpkin Magic Cake with Maple Cinnamon Whipped Cream

Prep: 25 mins **Cook:** 50 mins **Additional:** 30 mins **Total:** 1 hr 45 mins **Servings:** 9 **Yield:**

1 8-inch cake

Ingredients

- 1 cup all-purpose flour
- 2 tablespoons pumpkin pie spice
- 1 teaspoon sea salt
- 1 teaspoon ground cinnamon
- 1 ½ cups lukewarm milk
- 1 cup canned pumpkin
- 2 teaspoons vanilla extract

- 4 large eggs eggs, at room temperature, separated
- 1 cup white sugar
- ¼ cup brown sugar
- 1 tablespoon water
- ½ cup unsalted butter, melted
- 1 teaspoon cream of tartar

Maple Cinnamon Whipped Cream:

- 1 ¼ cups heavy whipping cream

- ¼ cup maple syrup
- ½ teaspoon ground cinnamon
- 1 pinch sea salt

Directions

Step 1

Preheat oven to 325 degrees F (165 degrees C). Grease an 8-inch baking pan.

Step 2

Whisk flour, pumpkin pie spice, 1 teaspoon salt, and 1 teaspoon cinnamon together in a bowl.

Step 3

Combine milk, pumpkin, and vanilla extract in a bowl.

Step 4

Place egg yolks, white sugar, brown sugar, and water in the bowl of a stand mixer. Beat on high speed until creamy. Reduce speed to low; add butter. Increase speed to medium; beat until light and fluffy. Reduce speed to low and add flour mixture in 3 batches, blending thoroughly after each addition and scraping down the sides of the bowl. Stir milk-pumpkin mixture slowly into the mixture until just combined; transfer to a separate bowl.

Step 5

Clean and dry out the bowl and beaters. Beat egg whites and cream of tartar on high speed until stiff peaks form. Fold 3/4 of the egg white mixture into the pumpkin mixture using a spatula; pour into the remaining egg whites, folding mixture in slowly until batter is smooth but still light and fluffy. Pour batter into the prepared pan.

Step 6

Bake in the preheated oven until edges are set and center still jiggles slightly, about 50 minutes. Let cool completely, at least 30 minutes.

Step 7

Beat heavy cream, maple syrup, 1/2 teaspoon cinnamon, and 1 pinch salt together in a bowl using an electric mixer until soft peaks form. Spread over cooled cake.

Nutrition Facts

Per Serving:

457.3 calories; protein 6.8g 14% DV; carbohydrates 51.4g 17% DV; fat 25.9g 40% DV; cholesterol 158.3mg 53% DV; sodium 362.2mg 15% DV.

283.2 calories; protein 4.3g 9% DV; carbohydrates 42.5g 14% DV; fat 11.1g 17% DV; cholesterol 62mg 21% DV; sodium 479.3mg 19% DV.

Pumpkin Crunch Cake with Cream Cheese Frosting

Prep: 15 mins **Cook:** 50 mins **Additional:** 1 hr **Total:** 2 hrs 5 mins **Servings:** 12 **Yield:** 12 servings

Ingredients

Cake:

- 1 (29 ounce) can pumpkin puree
- 1 (12 fluid ounce) can evaporated milk
- 1 cup white sugar
- 3 large eggs eggs
- 1 teaspoon ground cinnamon
- 1 (15.25 ounce) package yellow cake mix with pudding
- 1 cup chopped nuts
- 1 cup butter, melted

Frosting:

- 1 (8 ounce) package cream cheese, softened
- 1 cup confectioners' sugar
- ¾ cup frozen whipped topping (such as Cool Whip), thawed

Directions

Step 1

Preheat oven to 350 degrees F (175 degrees C). Line a 9x13-inch baking pan with parchment paper.

Step 2

Mix pumpkin, evaporated milk, sugar, eggs, and cinnamon together in a bowl; spread in the prepared baking pan. Pour cake mix on top. Pat chopped nuts into surface. Spoon melted butter evenly over nuts.

Step 3

Bake in the preheated oven until golden brown, 50 minutes to 1 hour. Allow cake to cool completely, about 1 hour. Turn over onto a baking sheet; remove parchment paper.

Step 4

Mix cream cheese, confectioners' sugar, and whipped topping together in a bowl. Spread onto cake.

Nutrition Facts

Per Serving:

622.1 calories; protein 9.1g 18% DV; carbohydrates 67.7g 22% DV; fat 36.9g 57% DV; cholesterol 116.8mg 39% DV; sodium 627mg 25% DV.

Pumpkin Pie Cake with Yellow Cake Mix

Servings: 24 **Yield:** 1 - 9x13 inch cake

Ingredients

- 1 (29 ounce) can pumpkin puree
- 1 (12 fluid ounce) can evaporated milk
- 3 large eggs eggs
- 1 cup white sugar
- 2 teaspoons ground cinnamon
- 1 teaspoon ground nutmeg
- ½ teaspoon ground ginger
- ½ teaspoon ground cloves
- 1 (18.25 ounce) package yellow cake mix
- 1 cup butter
- 1 cup chopped walnuts

Directions

Step 1

Preheat oven to 350 degrees F (175 degrees C). Line a 9 x 13 inch pan with parchment paper.

Step 2

In a large bowl, combine pumpkin, evaporated milk, eggs, sugar, cinnamon, nutmeg, ginger and cloves. Mix until smooth and pour into a 9x13 inch pan.

Step 3

Sprinkle dry cake mix over pumpkin mixture, then sprinkle chopped nuts and pat down gently. Melt butter or margarine and drizzle over cake.

Step 4

Bake at 350 degrees F (175 degrees C) for approximately 45 to 60 minutes. (Be sure to check the cake after 45 minutes because oven temperatures vary.)

Step 5

After cake cools, turn it upside down so the top of the cake will be the crust. Remove the parchment paper. Top with dessert topping (optional) before serving.

Nutrition Facts

Per Serving:

268 calories; protein 4g 8% DV; carbohydrates 30.5g 10% DV; fat 15.3g 24% DV; cholesterol 48.6mg 16% DV; sodium 303.2mg 12% DV.

Pumpkin Upside Down Cake

Prep: 20 mins **Cook:** 1 hr **Total:** 1 hr 20 mins **Servings:** 16 **Yield:** 1 - 9x13 inch cake

Ingredients

- 1 (29 ounce) can pumpkin
- 1 cup white sugar
- 3 large eggs eggs
- 1 (12 fluid ounce) can evaporated milk
- 1 tablespoon pumpkin pie spice
- 1 (18.25 ounce) package yellow cake mix
- 1 cup butter, melted
- 2 cups frozen whipped topping, thawed

Directions

Step 1

Preheat the oven to 350 degrees F (175 degrees C). Line a 9x13 inch baking pan with parchment paper or aluminum foil.

Step 2

In a large bowl, stir together the pumpkin, sugar and eggs. Mix in the evaporated milk and pumpkin pie spice; pour into the prepared pan.

Step 3

Sprinkle the dry cake mix over the pumpkin and then drizzle melted butter over the cake mix.

Step 4

Bake for 1 hour in the preheated oven, or until a knife inserted into the cake comes out clean. Cool, then invert onto a serving dish. Serve with whipped topping.

Nutrition Facts

Per Serving:

383 calories; protein 5g 10% DV; carbohydrates 46.7g 15% DV; fat 20.5g 32% DV; cholesterol 72.9mg 24% DV; sodium 457mg 18% DV.

Pumpkin Cheesecake I

Prep: 20 mins **Cook:** 50 mins **Total:** 1 hr 10 mins **Servings:** 16 **Yield:** 2 - 8 inch pie pans

Ingredients

- 2 (8 ounce) packages cream cheese
- ¾ cup white sugar
- 1 (15 ounce) can pumpkin puree
- 1 ¼ teaspoons ground cinnamon
- ½ teaspoon ground ginger
- ½ teaspoon ground nutmeg
- 2 large eggs eggs
- ¼ teaspoon salt
- 2 8" pie crust (blank)s prepared 8 inch pastry shells

Directions

Step 1

Preheat oven to 350 degrees F (175 degrees C).

Step 2

Beat together the cream cheese and the sugar, add the pumpkin and the spices. Beat in eggs one at a time. Add salt. Beat until creamy. Pour the batter evenly into the two pastry shells.

Step 3

Bake at 350 degrees F (175 degrees C) for 50 minutes or until the knife inserted in the center comes out clean. Let cool then top with whipped topping, if desired.

Nutrition Facts

Per Serving:

218 calories; protein 3.8g 8% DV; carbohydrates 18.8g 6% DV; fat 14.6g 23% DV; cholesterol 54mg 18% DV; sodium 274mg 11% DV.

Midnight Moon Cake

Servings: 12 **Yield:** 1 -9 inch round cake

Ingredients

- ½ cup shortening
- 1 ¼ cups white sugar
- 2 large eggs eggs
- 1 cup hot water
- ½ cup unsweetened cocoa powder
- 1 ½ cups sifted all-purpose flour
- ½ teaspoon salt
- 1 teaspoon baking soda
- 1 teaspoon baking powder
- 1 teaspoon vanilla extract
- 1 ½ cups confectioners' sugar
- 1 teaspoon lemon zest
- 2 fluid ounces lemon juice

Directions

Step 1

Preheat oven to 350 degrees F (175 degrees C). Grease and line with parchment paper one 9 inch round cake pan.

Step 2

Cream shortening, add white sugar gradually and cream until fluffy. Blend in the well beaten eggs.

Step 3

In a separate bowl, slowly add hot water to cocoa and mix until smooth, dissolving cocoa completely.

Step 4

In a third bowl, sift together the flour, salt, baking soda, and baking powder; add to creamed mixture alternately with the cocoa mixture. Blend in vanilla. Pour batter into one 9 inch round pan.

Step 5

Bake at 350 degrees F (175 degrees C) for 30 to 35 minutes or until cake tester comes out clean. Let cake cool then ice with Lemon Icing.

Step 6

To Make Icing: Combine confectioner's sugar with enough lemon juice to make the icing spreadable without being runny or stiff (about 1/4 cup). Stir in the grated zest. Pour icing over top of cake. See the full moon.

Nutrition Facts

Per Serving:

294.1 calories; protein 3.4g 7% DV; carbohydrates 50.3g 16% DV; fat 10g 15% DV; cholesterol 31mg 10% DV; sodium 255.4mg 10% DV.

The Popcorn Cake

Prep: 10 mins **Cook:** 10 mins **Additional:** 10 mins **Total:** 30 mins **Servings:** 14 **Yield:** 1 - 10 inch tube pan

Ingredients

- 14 cups popped popcorn
- 1 cup semisweet chocolate chips
- 1 cup peanuts
- ½ cup margarine
- ½ cup peanut butter
- 5 cups miniature marshmallows

Directions

Step 1

Line a 10 inch tube pan or other 12 cup pan with aluminum foil.

Step 2

In a very large bowl, combine popcorn, chocolate chips and peanuts and mix well.

Step 3

In a medium saucepan over low heat, melt margarine. Stir in peanut butter. Stir in marshmallows and continue stirring until marshmallows melt and the mixture is smooth. Remove from the heat. Stir marshmallow mixture into popcorn mixture until well coated.

Step 4

Press mixture into prepared pan. Allow to cool completely before removing and cutting into slices to serve.

Nutrition Facts

Per Serving:

356 calories; protein 6.4g 13% DV; carbohydrates 30.8g 10% DV; fat 24.6g 38% DV; cholesterolmg; sodium 259.3mg 10% DV.

Marie-Claude's Orange Cake

Prep: 1 hr 15 mins **Cook:** 30 mins **Total:** 1 hr 45 mins **Servings:** 12 **Yield:** 12 servings

Ingredients

- ⅜ cup vegetable oil
- 1 cup white sugar
- 2 large eggs eggs
- ½ cup plain yogurt
- 2 fruit, (2-5/8" dia, sphere)s oranges, zested and juiced
- 1 ½ cups all-purpose flour
- 1 teaspoon baking powder

Directions

Step 1

Preheat the oven to 375 degrees F (190 degrees C).

Step 2

In a medium bowl, mix together the vegetable oil, sugar and eggs. Stir in yogurt and orange zest. Combine the flour and baking powder; stir into the mixture just until blended. Pour the dough into a greased 9x13 inch baking pan.

Step 3

Bake for 30 minutes in the preheated oven, or until a knife inserted into the cake comes out clean. Poke holes in the cake with a knife, and pour the juice from the oranges over the cake slowly until it has all been absorbed.

Nutrition Facts

Per Serving:

213.3 calories; protein 3.5g 7% DV; carbohydrates 32.8g 11% DV; fat 8g 12% DV; cholesterol 31.6mg 11% DV; sodium 59.8mg 2% DV.

Pumpkin Roll with Toffee Cream Filling and Caramel Sauce

Servings: 12 **Yield:** 12 servings

Ingredients

- ¾ cup cake flour
- 1 ½ teaspoons ground cinnamon
- 1 ¼ teaspoons ground ginger
- ¾ teaspoon ground allspice
- 6 large egg yolks egg yolks
- 6 large egg whites egg whites
- ⅓ cup white sugar
- ⅓ cup packed light brown sugar
- ⅔ cup solid pack pumpkin puree
- ⅛ teaspoon salt
- ¼ cup confectioners' sugar for dusting
- 2 tablespoons dark rum
- 1 teaspoon unflavored gelatin
- 1 cup heavy whipping cream
- 3 tablespoons confectioners' sugar
- 10 tablespoons crushed toffee candy
- 1 (16 ounce) jar caramel ice cream topping, warmed
- ½ cup crushed toffee candy

Directions

Step 1

Preheat oven to 375 degrees F (190 degrees C). Spray a 15x10 inch baking sheet with vegetable oil spray. Sift flour, cinnamon, ginger and allspice into small bowl. Set aside.

Step 2

In a large bowl, beat egg yolks, 1/3 cup white sugar and 1/3 cup brown sugar until very thick, about 3 minutes with an electric mixer. On low speed, beat in pumpkin, then flour mixture. Using clean, dry beaters, in a large bowl, beat egg whites and salt until stiff but not dry. Fold egg whites into batter in 3 additions.

Step 3

Spread into prepared pan. Bake at 375 degrees F (190 degrees C) for 15 minutes, or until a toothpick inserted into cake comes out clean.

Step 4

Place smooth (not terry cloth) kitchen towel on work surface; dust generously with powdered sugar. Cut around pan edges to loosen cake. Turn cake out onto kitchen towel. Fold towel over 1 long side of cake. Starting at 1 long side, roll cake up in towel. Arrange cake seam side down and cool completely, about 1 hour.

Step 5

To make the filling: Pour 2 tablespoons rum into small heavy saucepan and sprinkle gelatin over. Let stand until gelatin softens, about 10 minutes. Stir over low heat just until gelatin dissolves, then remove from heat. In a large bowl, beat chilled whipping cream and 3 tablespoons powdered sugar until stiff peaks form. Beat in gelatin mixture. Fold in 6 tablespoons English toffee pieces.

Step 6

Unroll cake, sprinkle with 4 tablespoons English toffee pieces. Spread filling over. Starting at 1 long side and using kitchen towel as aid, roll up cake to enclose filling. Place cake seam side down on platter. (Can be prepared 1 day ahead.) Cover with foil and refrigerate.

Step 7

Trim ends of cake on slight diagonal. Dust cake with powdered sugar. Spoon some of the warm caramel sauce over top of cake. Sprinkle with 1/2 cup toffee. To serve, cut cake crosswise into 1 inch thick slices. Serve with remaining sauce.

Nutrition Facts

Per Serving:

428.7 calories; protein 5.2g 10% DV; carbohydrates 62.6g 20% DV; fat 17.7g 27% DV; cholesterol 147.8mg 49% DV; sodium 335.8mg 13% DV.

Pumpkin Upside-Down Cake

Prep: 15 mins **Cook:** 1 hr **Additional:** 1 hr 30 mins **Total:** 2 hrs 45 mins **Servings:** 24

Yield: 1 9x13-inch baking pan

Ingredients

- 1 (16 ounce) can pumpkin puree
- 1 (12 fluid ounce) can evaporated milk
- 1 cup white sugar
- 3 large eggs eggs
- 2 teaspoons ground cinnamon
- 1 (15.25 ounce) package yellow cake mix
- 1 cup chopped pecans
- 1 cup butter, melted
- 12 ounces nondairy whipped topping
- 1 (8 ounce) package cream cheese, softened
- 1 cup white sugar

Directions

Step 1

Preheat oven to 350 degrees F (175 degrees C). Line a 9x13-inch baking pan with parchment paper.

Step 2

Mix pumpkin puree, evaporated milk, 1 cup sugar, eggs, and cinnamon together in a bowl; pour into the prepared baking pan. Sprinkle cake mix over pumpkin mixture and top with pecans. Drizzle butter over pecan layer.

Step 3

Bake in the preheated oven until a toothpick inserted into the center comes out clean, about 1 hour. Cool cake in the pan, at least 30 minutes. Invert cake onto a flat plate.

Step 4

Mix whipped topping, cream cheese, and 1 cup white sugar together in a bowl; spread over the cake. Chill in the refrigerator, 1 to 2 hours. Cut into 1-inch squares.

Nutrition Facts

Per Serving:

344.7 calories; protein 4.1g 8% DV; carbohydrates 39.6g 13% DV; fat 20g 31% DV; cholesterol 58.8mg 20% DV; sodium 271.5mg 11% DV.

Spiderweb Pumpkin Cheesecake

Prep: 20 mins **Cook:** 50 mins **Additional:** 30 mins **Total:** 1 hr 40 mins **Servings:** 12 **Yield:**

12 servings

Ingredients

- 1 ¼ cups chocolate wafer crumbs
- ¼ cup butter, melted
- 3 (8 ounce) packages cream cheese, softened
- ¾ cup white sugar
- 3 large eggs eggs
- 1 ½ cups canned pumpkin pie filling
- 1 tablespoon cornstarch
- 1 cup sour cream
- 2 (1 ounce) squares semisweet chocolate
- 2 teaspoons vegetable oil

Directions

Step 1

Preheat oven to 350 degrees F (175 degrees C).

Step 2

Mix chocolate wafer crumbs and melted butter in a bowl; press onto the bottom of a 9-inch springform pan.

Step 3

Beat cream cheese and sugar with an electric mixer in a large bowl until smooth. Beat in eggs, one at a time, until just blended. Stir in pumpkin pie filling and cornstarch; pour over chocolate wafer crust.

Step 4

Bake in preheated oven until center is just set, 50 to 55 minutes.

Step 5

Spread sour cream over top of warm cheesecake; let cool.

Step 6

Melt chocolate and oil in a microwave-safe bowl in a microwave for 1 minute; stir until completely melted. Drizzle chocolate onto sour cream topping in a spiral pattern, starting from the center; draw a toothpick outward, from center to edges, through circles to form a web. Remove side of pan and serve.

Nutrition Facts

Per Serving:

454.8 calories; protein 7.9g 16% DV; carbohydrates 35.5g 12% DV; fat 32.6g 50% DV; cholesterol 126.9mg 42% DV; sodium 358.6mg 14% DV.

Double Layer Pumpkin Pie Cheesecake

Prep: 20 mins **Additional:** 4 hrs **Total:** 4 hrs 20 mins **Servings:** 8 **Yield:** 8 servings

Ingredients

- 1 (8 ounce) package cream cheese, softened
- 1 tablespoon milk
- 1 tablespoon white sugar
- 1 (8 ounce) container whipped topping (such as Cool Whip), thawed and divided
- 1 (6 ounce) graham cracker crust (such as Nabisco Honey Maid)
- 1 (15 ounce) can pumpkin puree
- 1 cup milk
- 2 (3.4 ounce) packages instant vanilla pudding mix
- 1 teaspoon ground cinnamon
- ½ teaspoon ground ginger

- ¼ teaspoon ground cloves

Directions

Step 1

Beat cream cheese, 1 tablespoon milk, and sugar together in a large bowl with a whisk until blended. Stir in half of whipped topping; spread into crust.

Step 2

Whisk pumpkin puree, 1 cup milk, pudding mix, cinnamon, ginger, and ground cloves together in a bowl until mixture is thick and blended. Spread over cream cheese mixture.

Step 3

Chill in the refrigerator until set, about 4 hours. Remove from the refrigerator; top with remaining whipped topping before serving.

Nutrition Facts

Per Serving:

421.2 calories; protein 5g 10% DV; carbohydrates 50.9g 16% DV; fat 23.1g 36% DV; cholesterol 33.4mg 11% DV; sodium 696.3mg 28% DV.

Trick or Treat Cheesecake

Prep: 20 mins **Cook:** 50 mins **Additional:** 9 hrs **Total:** 10 hrs 10 mins **Servings:** 12 **Yield:**

12 servings

Ingredients

- cooking spray

Crust:

- 25 cookies chocolate sandwich cookies (such as Oreo), crushed
- ⅓ cup white sugar
- ⅓ cup melted butter

Filling:

- 2 (8 ounce) packages cream cheese, softened
- 1 (14 ounce) can sweetened condensed milk
- 3 large eggs eggs
- 20 mini chocolate-coated caramel-peanut nougat candy bars (such as Snickers), cut into quarters
- 2 teaspoons vanilla extract

Directions

Step 1

Preheat oven to 300 degrees F (150 degrees C). Place a shallow pan 1/2-full with water on the lower oven rack to minimize cracking in the cheesecake. Spray the inside of a 9-inch springform pan with cooking spray and line with parchment paper.

Step 2

Mix chocolate sandwich cookies, sugar, and butter together in a bowl; press into the bottom of the prepared pan.

Step 3

Beat cream cheese and sweetened condensed milk together in a separate bowl using an electric mixer until smooth; beat in eggs, 1 at a time, until just blended. Stir candy bars and vanilla extract into cream cheese mixture; pour over crust.

Step 4

Bake in the preheated oven until edges are set and center is still slightly soft, about 50 minutes. Turn off oven, leaving door open, and cool cheesecake in oven, at least 1 hour. Run a knife or spatula around the edges to loosen cheesecake; refrigerate in the pan until set, 8 hours or overnight.

Nutrition Facts

Per Serving:

490.4 calories; protein 9.3g 19% DV; carbohydrates 48.5g 16% DV; fat 29.8g 46% DV; cholesterol 114.2mg 38% DV; sodium 343.4mg 14% DV.

Frankenstein Ice Cream Cake

Prep: 30 mins **Additional:** 6 hrs 30 mins **Total:** 7 hrs **Servings:** 16 **Yield:** 1 loaf cake

Ingredients

- ½ gallon mint chocolate chip ice cream
- 2 cups heavy whipping cream
- ½ cup white sugar
- 1 pouch whipped cream stabilizer (such as Dr. Oetker Whip It)
- 2 teaspoons vanilla extract
- 1 drop green food coloring, or as desired
- 2 cups crushed chocolate sandwich cookies (such as Oreo)
- ½ cup melted butter
- 1 tablespoon hot fudge sauce, or as needed
- 2 tablespoons chocolate sprinkles, or as desired
- 2 cookies chocolate sandwich cookies (such as Oreo)

Directions

Step 1

Put ice cream in the refrigerator to soften while you make whipped cream frosting.

Step 2

Beat cream in a bowl using an electric mixer until stiff peaks almost form. Add white sugar, whipped cream stabilizer, vanilla extract, and green food coloring to whipped cream; beat until stiff peaks form.

Step 3

Scoop softened ice cream into a large bowl; stir until a uniform consistency is reached. The ice cream shouldn't be completely melted, but firm enough to hold form. Scoop ice cream into the loaf pan and spread evenly using a spatula, trying to avoid creating air bubbles.

Step 4

Mix crushed cookies and melted butter together in a bowl. Pat cookie mixture the ice cream for the "hair"; freeze for 5 hours. Run a knife along the edges of the pan and carefully flip it upside-down over a cake platter. Return cake to the freezer until firm, at least 30 minutes.

Step 5

Spread whipped cream evenly over the top and sides of cake. Freeze cake until solid, about 1 hour more.

Step 6

Spoon hot fudge sauce onto the cake creating "eyes", a "mouth", and "hairline"; top hot fudge areas with sprinkles. Place 1 cookie on each side of the bottom of the cake for the "neck bolts". Freeze cake until ready to eat.

Nutrition Facts

Per Serving:

541.9 calories; protein 6.3g 13% DV; carbohydrates 42g 14% DV; fat 39.2g 60% DV; cholesterol 150.4mg 50% DV; sodium 174.8mg 7% DV.

Halloween Layer Cake

Prep: 30 mins **Cook:** 30 mins **Total:** 1 hr **Servings:** 24 **Yield:** 2 - 9 inch round cakes

Ingredients

- 1 ¾ cups cake flour
- 1 teaspoon baking soda
- 1 teaspoon salt
- 1 ½ cups white sugar
- ⅓ cup shortening
- 1 cup buttermilk
- 3 large egg whites egg whites
- 4 (1 ounce) squares unsweetened chocolate, melted
- 1 teaspoon butter
- ⅓ cup butter, softened
- 1 ½ tablespoons orange zest
- 1 teaspoon lemon zest
- ¼ teaspoon salt
- 1 egg yolk
- 4 cups sifted confectioners' sugar
- 1 tablespoon orange juice
- 2 teaspoons lemon juice

Directions

Step 1

Preheat oven to 350 degrees F (175 degrees C). Line the bottoms of two 8 or 9 inch round cake pans with parchment paper.

Step 2

Sift together the flour, baking soda, salt, and white sugar.

Step 3

Beat shortening until light and fluffy. Mix in dry ingredients. Add 3/4 cup of buttermilk and mix until all flour is dampened. Then beat with electric mixer. Add egg whites, melted chocolate, and remaining buttermilk, beat well and pour batter into prepared pans.

Step 4

Bake at 350 degrees F (175 degrees C) for 30 minutes. When cake is cool frost between layer and over top and sides with Golden Orange Frosting. Mark outlines of Halloween cats and bats by lightly pressing paper cut-outs into frosting, then removing paper. Melt 1 square unsweetened chocolate with 1 tsp. butter. Using a brush, fill in the outlines with the chocolate mixture.

Step 5

To Make Golden Orange Frosting: Cream together butter, orange rind, lemon rind, and salt. Add egg yolk and mix well. Add confectioners sugar, alternately with orange juice and lemon juice, beating well after each addition. Makes 2 cups frosting, or enough to cover tops and sides of two 9 inch layers.

Nutrition Facts

Per Serving:

249.2 calories; protein 2.4g 5% DV; carbohydrates 43.6g 14% DV; fat 8.4g 13% DV; cholesterol 16.2mg 5% DV; sodium 212.5mg 9% DV.

Dairy-Free Halloween Black Cake

Prep: 15 mins **Cook:** 20 mins **Total:** 35 mins **Servings:** 8 **Yield:** 1 9-inch cake pan

Ingredients

- 1 ½ cups all-purpose flour
- 1 cup white sugar
- ¾ cup chocolate chips
- ⅔ cup unsweetened cocoa powder
- 2 teaspoons baking soda
- 1 teaspoon salt

- 1 cup cold brew coffee with grounds
- ¾ cup pumpkin puree
- 2 tablespoons vegetable oil
- 2 teaspoons vanilla extract
- 2 tablespoons white vinegar

Directions

Step 1

Preheat oven to 350 degrees F (175 degrees C).

Step 2

Mix flour, sugar, chocolate chips, cocoa powder, baking soda, and salt together in a 9-inch cake pan. Add cold brew, pumpkin puree, oil, and vanilla extract and mix thoroughly. Stir vinegar in until just combined.

Step 3

Bake in the preheated oven until a toothpick inserted into the center comes out clean, 20 to 30 minutes.

Nutrition Facts

Per Serving:

315.3 calories; protein 4.8g 10% DV; carbohydrates 58.7g 19% DV; fat 9.4g 15% DV; cholesterolmg; sodium 665.1mg 27% DV.

Halloween Cheesecake

Prep: 15 mins **Cook:** 40 mins **Additional:** 1 hr 30 mins **Total:** 2 hrs 25 mins **Servings:** 10

Yield: 1 9-inch cheesecake

Ingredients

Crust:

- 16 cookies chocolate sandwich cookies (such as Oreo)
- 5 tablespoons butter, melted
- 3 tablespoons white sugar

Filling:

- 2 (8 ounce) packages cream cheese, softened
- ½ cup white sugar
- 2 large eggs eggs
- ½ cup sour cream
- 1 teaspoon vanilla extract

Directions

Step 1

Preheat the oven to 350 degrees F (175 degrees C). Butter a 9-inch springform pan.

Step 2

Process cookies in a food processor until reduced to coarse crumbs. Reserve 1 tablespoon for decoration; combine the rest with butter and sugar. Spread mixture onto the bottom of the prepared pan, pressing down firmly to form a crust.

Step 3

Bake in the preheated oven until set, 8 to 10 minutes. Remove; reduce oven temperature to 325 degrees F (163 degrees C).

Step 4

Beat cream cheese and sugar together using an electric mixer until creamy, about 2 minutes. Add eggs one at a time, mixing well after each addition. Add sour cream and vanilla extract. Blend well. Pour filling into the cooled crust.

Step 5

Bake in the preheated oven until center is nearly set, about 30 minutes. Turn off oven and leave cheesecake inside to cool, at least 30 minutes. Continue cooling in the refrigerator for at least 1 hour. Decorate with reserved cookie crumbs.

Nutrition Facts

Per Serving:

375.2 calories; protein 5.9g 12% DV; carbohydrates 27g 9% DV; fat 27.8g 43% DV; cholesterol 106.8mg 36% DV; sodium 270.9mg 11% DV.

Chocolate Magic Cake

Prep: 20 mins **Cook:** 50 mins **Additional:** 30 mins **Total:** 1 hr 40 mins **Servings:** 10 **Yield:** 10 servings

Ingredients

- ⅔ cup unsweetened cocoa powder
- ⅓ cup all-purpose flour
- 2 teaspoons instant espresso powder
- ¾ teaspoon sea salt
- 4 large eggs eggs at room temperature, separated
- 1 cup white sugar
- 1 tablespoon water
- ½ cup unsalted butter, melted
- 2 teaspoons vanilla extract
- 2 cups whole milk, lukewarm
- 1 teaspoon cream of tartar

Directions

Step 1

Preheat oven to 325 degrees F (165 degrees C). Grease an 8-inch baking pan.

Step 2

Whisk cocoa powder, flour, espresso powder, and salt together in a bowl.

Step 3

Combine egg yolks, white sugar, and water in the bowl of a stand mixer. Beat on high speed until eggs are light and creamy, about 2 minutes. Reduce speed to low and add butter and vanilla extract. Increase speed to medium; beat until light and fluffy, about 1 minute. Reduce speed to low and add the cocoa mixture in 3 batches, mixing thoroughly after each addition and scraping down the sides of the bowl. Stir milk slowly into the batter until well combined. Pour chocolate batter into a separate bowl.

Step 4

Clean and dry out bowl and beaters. Beat egg whites and cream of tartar together on high speed until stiff peaks form. Fold 3/4 of the egg white mixture into the chocolate batter using a spatula; pour back into the egg white bowl, folding mixture in slowly until batter is smooth but still light and fluffy. Pour batter into the prepared pan.

Step 5

Bake in the preheated oven until edges are set and center still jiggles slightly, about 50 minutes. Let cake cool completely, at least 30 minutes.

Nutrition Facts

Per Serving:

248.6 calories; protein 5.8g 12% DV; carbohydrates 29g 9% DV; fat 13.6g 21% DV; cholesterol 103.7mg 35% DV; sodium 182.4mg 7% DV.

Potato Chocolate Cake

Prep: 1 hr **Cook:** 45 mins **Additional:** 15 mins **Total:** 2 hrs **Servings:** 24 **Yield:** 1 - 9x13 inch pan

Ingredients

- 1 cup margarine
- 2 cups white sugar
- 4 large eggs eggs
- 2 (1 ounce) squares unsweetened chocolate, melted
- 1 teaspoon vanilla extract
- 1 cup prepared instant mashed potatoes
- 2 cups sifted all-purpose flour
- 1 teaspoon baking soda
- 1 teaspoon salt
- ¾ cup buttermilk

Directions

Step 1

Preheat oven to 375 degrees F (190 degrees C). Grease and flour a 9x13 inch pan. Sift together the flour, baking soda and salt. Set aside.

Step 2

In a large bowl, cream together the margarine and sugar until light and fluffy. Beat in the eggs one at a time. Stir in the melted chocolate, vanilla and mashed potatoes. Beat in the flour mixture alternately with the buttermilk, mixing just until incorporated.

Step 3

Pour batter into prepared pan. Bake in the preheated oven for 45 minutes, or until a toothpick inserted into the center of the cake comes out clean. Allow to cool.

Nutrition Facts

Per Serving:

204.9 calories; protein 2.9g 6% DV; carbohydrates 26.8g 9% DV; fat 10.1g 16% DV; cholesterol 32.5mg 11% DV; sodium 271.8mg 11% DV.

White Chocolate Bubbling Cauldrons

Prep: 1 hr **Cook:** 30 mins **Additional:** 10 mins **Total:** 1 hr 40 mins **Servings:** 6 **Yield:** 6 8-ounce ramekins

Ingredients

- 1 pound bittersweet chocolate, chopped
- 1 (12 ounce) package black confectioners' coating (such as black Wilton Candy Melts)
- 1 cup unsalted butter, softened
- ½ cup white sugar
- 3 large eggs eggs, room temperature
- 3 large egg yolks egg yolks, room temperature
- 1 cup all-purpose flour
- 1 cup ground toasted pecans
- 1 teaspoon vanilla extract
- 1 (12 ounce) package green confectioners' coating (such as green Wilton Candy Melts)
- 1 (12 ounce) package white confectioners' coating (such as white Wilton Candy Melts)
- ¾ cup heavy whipping cream
- 2 ounces bittersweet chocolate, grated
- 6 pretzels chocolate-covered pretzel sticks

Directions

Step 1

Preheat oven to 350 degrees F (175 degrees C). Generously butter six 8-ounce ramekins and place on baking sheet.

Step 2

Melt 1 pound chopped bittersweet chocolate in a plastic or glass bowl in microwave oven on low, stirring every 30 seconds, or in the top of a double-boiler over gently simmering water. Remove melted chocolate from heat and set aside to cool. It should be room temperature but still fluid.

Step 3

Melt black confectioners' coating in a separate large plastic or glass bowl in microwave oven on low, stirring every 30 seconds, until coating is melted, warm, and smooth. Keep candy warm.

Step 4

Beat butter and sugar in a bowl using an electric mixer fitted with a whisk attachment on high speed until mixture is light and fluffy, about 5 minutes. Add eggs one at a time, allowing each egg to blend into the butter mixture before adding the next. Beat in egg yolks one at a time. Continue mixing until batter is thick and lemon-colored, about 3 minutes.

Step 5

Pour cooled melted chocolate into butter mixture and mix on low speed, stopping to scrape down sides of bowl, until fully combined. Beat flour, ground pecans, and vanilla extract into chocolate mixture and continue to mix just until batter comes together. Divide batter among prepared ramekins.

Step 6

Bake in preheated oven for 15 minutes. Remove tray from oven. Carefully place 2 or 3 green candy pieces and 1 white candy piece (or more white than green, if desired) in the center of each half-baked cake. Return cakes to oven and bake for another 10 to 15 minutes, or until a knife inserted in the side comes out clean (do not pierce the centers). Let cakes cool in ramekins for 10 minutes.

Step 7

Melt 2 or 3 pieces of the green candy in a small microwave-safe bowl in microwave set on low, stirring every 30 seconds, until green candy is warm and smooth. Let cool until room temperature but still fluid. Whip the heavy cream in a bowl and gently fold cooled green candy melts into the whipped cream.

Step 8

Gently unmold cakes onto baking sheet. Carefully dip cakes into black candy coating, or pour it over the cakes to coat. Sprinkle grated chocolate onto a serving platter and place cakes onto the grated chocolate. Spoon a dollop of green whipped cream on top of each cake. Pierce each cake with a chocolate-covered pretzel stick, allowing the bubbling cauldrons to ooze their green and white candy filling. Serve immediately.

Nutrition Facts

Per Serving:

2117.8 calories; protein 25.4g 51% DV; carbohydrates 193.1g 62% DV; fat 141.7g 218% DV; cholesterol 356.9mg 119% DV; sodium 275.1mg 11% DV.

Super Easy Halloween Cake

Prep: 10 mins **Cook:** 25 mins **Total:** 35 mins **Servings:** 24 **Yield:** 1 9x13-inch pan

Ingredients

- 1 (18.25 ounce) package yellow cake mix
- 1 (15 ounce) can pumpkin puree
- 2 large eggs eggs
- 1 cup semisweet chocolate chips

Directions

Step 1

Preheat oven to 350 degrees F (175 degrees C). Grease a 9x13-inch baking pan.

Step 2

Beat cake mix, pumpkin puree, and eggs together in a bowl using an electric mixer until batter is smooth, about 2 minutes. Fold chocolate chips into batter; pour into the prepared baking pan.

Step 3

Bake in the preheated oven until a toothpick inserted into the center comes out clean, 25 to 30 minutes.

Nutrition Facts

Per Serving:

138.6 calories; protein 2g 4% DV; carbohydrates 22.7g 7% DV; fat 5.1g 8% DV; cholesterol 15.9mg 5% DV; sodium 190.9mg 8% DV.

Smart Cookie's Spiderweb Pumpkin Cheesecake

Prep: 20 mins **Cook:** 1 hr 20 mins **Additional:** 7 hrs **Total:** 8 hrs 40 mins **Servings:** 12

Yield: 1 (10-inch) cheesecake

Ingredients

Gingersnap and Pecan Crust:

- cooking spray
- 48 eaches gingersnap cookies
- ½ cup pecan pieces
- ½ cup salted butter, melted

Pumpkin Cheesecake:

- 4 (8 ounce) packages cream cheese, at room temperature
- 1 ½ cups white sugar
- 4 eaches eggs, at room temperature
- 2 teaspoons vanilla extract
- 1 cup canned pumpkin puree
- 1 ½ teaspoons pumpkin pie spice blend

Directions

Step 1

Preheat the oven to 350 degrees F (175 degrees C). Spray a 10-inch springform pan with cooking spray and wrap the outside with foil.

Step 2

Pulse gingersnap cookies into fine crumbs in a food processor. Transfer to a medium mixing bowl. Pulse pecans in the same food processor bowl until finely ground. Add to the cookie mixture and mix in melted butter.

Step 3

Press the cookie and pecan mixture into the bottom and halfway up the sides of the springform pan.

Step 4

Bake in the preheated oven until golden brown on the edges, about 10 minutes. Cool on a wire rack. Reduce the oven temperature to 300 degrees F (150 degrees C).

Step 5

Beat cream cheese with sugar in the bowl of a stand mixer fitted with the paddle attachment, stopping occasionally to scrape the sides of the bowl, until smooth and creamy, about 3 minutes. Add eggs 1 at a time, beating just until combined and scraping the sides of the bowl after each addition. Beat in vanilla extract.

Step 6

Pour about 1/2 of the batter into a different bowl and set aside.

Step 7

Add pumpkin puree and pumpkin spice to the batter in the stand mixer bowl and mix until combined.

Step 8

Transfer 1/4 cup of the plain batter into a piping bag or plastic storage bag. Spread the rest over the pie crust. Top with the pumpkin cheesecake batter.

Step 9

Pipe remaining plain batter into 5 concentric circles on the top of the cheesecake. Drag the tip of a toothpick or small knife out from the center of the batter to the edge, wiping it down between each pull, to create a spider web effect.

Step 10

Place the springform pan in the bottom of a roasting pan; fill roasting pan halfway up with warm water to create a water bath.

Step 11

Carefully transfer cheesecake to the oven and bake until edges are set, top is no longer shiny, and center is still a little jiggly, about 1 hour and 10 minutes.

Step 12

Turn the oven off and prop the door open at least 4 inches. Leave the cheesecake in the oven for an additional 30 minutes.

Step 13

Remove cheesecake from the oven and water bath. Run a knife around the edge to prevent sticking and cool on a cooling rack for 30 minutes more. Cover loosely and chill for at least 6 hours, or overnight.

Step 14

Run a knife around the edge of the pan and carefully remove the sides of the springform pan. Slice and serve.

Nutrition Facts

Per Serving:

606.4 calories; protein 9.3g 19% DV; carbohydrates 48.1g 16% DV; fat 43.2g 66% DV; cholesterol 157mg 52% DV; sodium 439.9mg 18% DV.

Pumpkin Cake I

Prep: 15 mins **Cook:** 1 hr **Additional:** 5 mins **Total:** 1 hr 20 mins **Servings:** 12 **Yield:**

1 10-inch bundt cake

Ingredients

- 1 cup vegetable oil
- 3 large eggs eggs
- 1 (15 ounce) can pumpkin puree
- 1 teaspoon vanilla extract
- 2 ½ cups white sugar

- 2 ½ cups all-purpose flour
- 1 teaspoon baking soda
- 1 teaspoon ground nutmeg
- 1 teaspoon ground allspice
- 1 teaspoon ground cinnamon

- 1 teaspoon ground cloves
- ¼ teaspoon salt
- 1 cup chopped walnuts

Directions

Step 1

Preheat oven to 350 degrees F (175 degrees C). Grease one 10-inch bundt or tube pan.

Step 2

Blend oil, beaten eggs, pumpkin and vanilla together.

Step 3

Sift the flour, sugar, baking soda, ground nutmeg, ground allspice, ground cinnamon, ground cloves and salt together. Add the flour mixture to the pumpkin mixture and mix until just combined. If desired, stir in some chopped nuts. Pour batter into the prepared pan.

Step 4

Bake in preheated oven until a toothpick inserted in the middle comes out clean, about 1 hour. Let cake cool in pan for 5 minutes, then turn out onto a plate and sprinkle with confectioners' sugar.

Nutrition Facts

Per Serving:

517.3 calories; protein 6.2g 12% DV; carbohydrates 66.4g 21% DV; fat 26.6g 41% DV; cholesterol 46.5mg 16% DV; sodium 257.7mg 10% DV.